3 9047 00026394 3

• THE COLLECTED POEMS OF GEORGE OPPEN

· THE COLLECTED POEMS OF GEORGE OPPEN

● A NEW DIRECTIONS BOOK

ACKNOWLEDGMENTS
Some of the poems in this book first appeared in Ezra Pound's *Active Anthology, The American Poetry Review, Exiles, Hound and Horn, The Iowa Review, Ironwood, Maps, Massachusetts Review, The Nation, The Objectivist Anthology, Paris Review, Red Cedar Review, San Francisco Review, Stony Brook, Sumac,* and *West End,* among others.

The poem "Bahamas" was published originally in *The New Yorker.* "Philai te kou philai," "Psalm," "The Forms of Love," "Giovanni's 'Rape of the Sabine Women' at Wildenstein's," "Street," "Primitive," "Guest Room," "The People, the People," "Historic Pun," "A Theological Definition," and "Ballad" all first appeared in *Poetry.*

In *Of Being Numerous,* phrases, comments, cadences of speech occur, in some instances without quotation marks, which are derived from friends, among them: Rachel Blau, John Crawford, Steven Schneider, Armand Schwerner, Phyllis Rivera, Chestina Torrey. The entire sixteenth section of the title poem is quoted from Søren Kierkegaard.

Seascape: Needle's Eye was first published by Dan Gerber at The Sumac Press, Freemont, Michigan, in 1972.

Manufactured in the United States of America
First published clothbound in 1975
Published simultaneously in Canada by McClelland & Stewart, Ltd.

Library of Congress Cataloging in Publication Data

Oppen, George.
   The collected poems of George Oppen
   (A New Directions Book)
   Includes index.
PS3529.P54   1975   811'.5'2   75-6965
ISBN: 0-8112-0583-5

New Directions Books are published for James Laughlin by New Directions Publishing Corporation, 333 Sixth Avenue, New York 10014

76-04890

• CONTENTS

Discrete Series (1932–1934)   1

The Materials (1962)   15

This in Which (1965)   69

Of Being Numerous (1968)   145

Seascape: Needle's Eye (1972)   203

Myth of the Blaze (new poems, 1972–1975)   231

Index of titles and first lines   257

For Mary

whose words in this book are entangled
inextricably among my own

- DISCRETE SERIES

The knowledge not of sorrow, you were
        saying, but of boredom
Is—aside from reading speaking
        smoking——
Of what, Maude Blessingbourne it was,
        wished to know when, having risen,
"approached the window as if to see
        what really was going on";
And saw rain falling, in the distance
        more slowly,
The road clear from her past the window-
        glass——
Of the world, weather-swept, with which
        one shares the century.

1

White. From the
Under arm of T

The red globe.

Up
Down. Round
Shiny fixed
Alternatives

From the quiet

Stone floor . . .

2

    Thus
Hides the

Parts—the prudery
Of Frigidaire, of
Soda-jerking——

Thus

Above the

Plane of lunch, of wives
Removes itself
(As soda-jerking from
the private act

Of
Cracking eggs);

big-Business

The evening, water in a glass
Thru which our car runs on a higher road.

Over what has the air frozen?

Nothing can equal in polish and obscured
      origin that dark instrument
A car
      (Which.
Ease; the hand on the sword-hilt

Her ankles are watches
(Her arm-pits are causeways for water)

When she steps
She walks on a sphere

Walks on the carpet, dressing.
Brushing her hair

Her movement accustomed, abstracted,
Declares this morning a woman's
"My hair, scalp——"

1

The three wide
Funnels raked aft, and the masts slanted

      the
Deck-hand slung in a bosun's chair
Works on this 20th century chic and
       efficiency
Not evident at "The Sailor's Rest."

2

The lights, paving——
This important device
Of a race

Remains till morning.

           Burns
Against the wall.
He has chosen a place
With the usual considerations,
Without stating them.
Buildings.

The mast
Inaudibly soars; bole-like, tapering:
Sail flattens from it beneath the wind.
The limp water holds the boat's round
                         sides. Sun
Slants dry light on the deck.
                    Beneath us glide
Rocks, sands, and unrimmed holes.

Closed car—closed in glass——
At the curb,
Unapplied and empty:
A thing among others
Over which clouds pass and the
                    alteration of lighting,
An overstatement
Hardly an exterior.
Moving in traffic
This thing is less strange——
Tho the face, still within it,
Between glasses—place, over which
                    time passes—a false light.

· 6

Who comes is occupied
Toward the chest (in the crowd moving
        opposite
Grasp of me)
              In firm overalls
The middle-aged man sliding
Levers in the steam-shovel cab,——
Lift (running cable) and swung, back
Remotely respond to the gesture before last
Of his arms fingers continually——
Turned with the cab. But if I (how goes
        it?)——
                The asphalt edge
Loose on the plateau,
Horse's classic height cartless
See electric flash of streetcar,
The fall is falling from electric burst.

PARTY ON SHIPBOARD

Wave in the round of the port-hole
Springs, passing,—arm waved,
Shrieks, unbalanced by the motion——
Like the sea incapable of contact
Save in incidents (the sea is not
        water)
Homogeneously automatic—a green capped
        white is momentarily a half mile
            out——
The shallow surface of the sea, this,
Numerously—the first drinks——
The sea is a constant weight
In its bed. They pass, however, the sea
Freely tumultuous.

This land:
The hills, round under straw;
A house

With rigid trees

And flaunts
A family laundry,
And the glass of windows

Semaphoring chorus,
The width of the stage. The usher from it:
Seats' curving rows two sides by distant
        phosphor. And those 'filled';
Man and wife, removing gloves
Or overcoat. Still faces already lunar.

The edge of the ocean,
The shore: here
Somebody's lawn,
By the water.

Tug against the river——
Motor turning, lights
In the fast water off the bow-wave:
Passes slowly.

She lies, hip high,
On a flat bed
While the after-
Sun passes.

Plant, I breathe——
                    O Clearly,
Eyes legs arms hands fingers,
Simple legs in silk.

Civil war photo:
Grass near the lens;
Man in the field
In silk hat. Daylight.
The cannon of that day
In our parks.

As I saw
There
Year ago——
If there's a bird
On the cobbles;
One I've not seen

Bolt
In the frame
Of the building——
A ship
Grounds
Her immense keel
Chips
A stone
Under fifteen feet
Of harbor
Water——
The fiber of this tree
Is live wood
Running into the
Branches and leaves
In the air.

From this distance thinking toward you,
Time is recession

Movement of no import
Not encountering you

Save the pulse cumulates a past
And your pulse separate doubly.

Town, a town,
But location
Over which the sun as it comes to it;
Which cools, houses and lamp-posts,
        during the night, with the roads——
Inhabited partly by those
Who have been born here,
Houses built——. From a train one sees
        him in the morning, his morning;
Him in the afternoon, straightening——
People everywhere, time and the work
        pauseless:
One moves between reading and re-reading,
The shape is a moment.
From a crowd a white powdered face,
Eyes and mouth making three——
Awaited—locally—a date.

Near your eyes——
Love at the pelvis
Reaches the generic, gratuitous
                (Your eyes like snail-tracks)

Parallel emotions,
We slide in separate hard grooves
Bowstrings to bent loins,
                Self moving
Moon, mid-air.

Fragonard,
Your spiral women
By a fountain

'1732'

Your picture lasts thru us

                its air
Thick with succession of civilizations;
And the women.

No interval of manner
Your body in the sun.
You? A solid, this that the dress
                insisted,
Your face unaccented, your mouth a mouth?
                Practical knees:
It is you who truly
Excel the vegetable,
The fitting of grasses—more bare than
                that.
Pointedly bent, your elbow on a car-edge
Incognito as summer
Among mechanics.

'O city ladies'
Your coats wrapped,
Your hips a possession

Your shoes arched
Your walk is sharp

Your breasts
         Pertain to lingerie

The fields are road-sides,
Rooms outlast you.

Bad times:
The cars pass
By the elevated posts
And the movie sign.
A man sells post-cards.

It brightens up into the branches
And against the same buildings

A morning:
His job is as regular.

On the water, solid——
The singleness of a toy——

A tug with two barges.

O what O what will
Bring us back to
Shore,
         the shore

Coiling a rope on the steel deck

DRAWING

Not by growth
    But the
Paper, turned, contains
This entire volume

Deaths everywhere——
The world too short for trend is land——
       In the mouths,
            Rims

In this place, two geraniums
In your window-box
Are his life's eyes.

Written structure,
Shape of art,
More formal
Than a field would be
(existing in it)——
Her pleasure's
Looser;
'O—'

      'Tomorrow?'—

Successive
Happenings
(the telephone)

- **THE MATERIALS**

*We awake in the same moment to
ourselves and to things.*

                    —Maritain

*They fed their hearts on fantasies
And their hearts have become savage.*

• ECLOGUE

The men talking
Near the room's center. They have said
More than they had intended.

Pinpointing in the uproar
Of the living room

An assault
On the quiet continent.

Beyond the window
Flesh and rock and hunger

Loose in the night sky
Hardened into soil

Tilting of itself to the sun once more, small
Vegetative leaves
And stems taking place

Outside — O small ones,
To be born!

● IMAGE OF THE ENGINE

1

Likely as not a ruined head gasket
Spitting at every power stroke, if not a crank shaft
Bearing knocking at the roots of the thing like a pile-driver:
A machine involved with itself, a concentrated
Hot lump of a machine
Geared in the loose mechanics of the world with the valves
        jumping
And the heavy frenzy of the pistons. When the thing stops,
Is stopped, with the last slow cough
In the manifold, the flywheel blundering
Against compression, stopping, finally
Stopped, compression leaking
From the idle cylinders will one imagine
Then because he can imagine
That squeezed from the cooling steel
There hovers in that moment, wraith-like and like a plume
        of steam, an aftermath,
A still and quiet angel of knowledge and of comprehension.

2

Endlessly, endlessly,
The definition of mortality

The image of the engine

That stops.
We cannot live on that.
I know that no one would live out
Thirty years, fifty years if the world were ending
With his life.
The machine stares out,
Stares out
With all its eyes

Thru the glass
With the ripple in it, past the sill
Which is dusty — If there is someone
In the garden!
Outside, and so beautiful.

3

What ends
Is that.
       Even companionship
Ending.

'I want to ask if you remember
When we were happy! As tho all travels

Ended untold, all embarkations
Foundered.

4

On that water
Grey with morning
The gull will fold its wings
And sit. And with its two eyes
There as much as anything
Can watch a ship and all its hallways
And all companions sink.

5

Also he has set the world
In their hearts. From lumps, chunks,

We are locked out: like children, seeking love
At last among each other. With their first full strength
The young go search for it,

Native in the native air.
But even in the beautiful bony children
Who arise in the morning have left behind
Them worn and squalid toys in the trash

Which is a grimy death of love. The lost
Glitter of the stores!
The streets of stores!
Crossed by the streets of stores
And every crevice of the city leaking
Rubble: concrete, conduit, pipe, a crumbling
Rubble of our roots

                But they will find
In flood, storm, ultimate mishap:
Earth, water, the tremendous
Surface, the heart thundering
Absolute desire.

• POPULATION

Like a flat sea,
Here is where we are, the empty reaches
Empty of ourselves

Where dark, light, sound
Shatter the mind born
Alone to ocean

Save we are
A crowd, a population, those
Born, those not yet dead, the moment's

Populace, sea-borne and violent, finding
Incredibly under the sense the rough deck
Inhabited, and what it always was.

• RESORT

There's a volcano snow-capped in the air some twenty miles
        from here
In clear lit air,
There is a tree in leaf here —

In dream an old man walking,
An old man's rounded head
Abruptly mine

Self-involved, strange, alien,
The familiar flesh
Walking. I saw his neck, his cheek

And called, called:
Called several times.

• SOLUTION

The puzzle assembled
At last in the box lid showing a green
Hillside, a house,
A barn and man
And wife and children,
All of it polychrome,
Lucid, backed by the blue
Sky. The jigsaw of cracks
Crazes the landscape but there is no gap,
No actual edged hole
Nowhere the wooden texture of the table top
Glares out of scale in the picture,
Sordid as cellars, as bare foundations:
There is no piece missing. The puzzle is complete
Now in its red and green and brown.

● TRAVELOGUE

But no screen would show
The light, the volume
Of the moment, or our decisions

In the dugouts, roaring
Downstream with the mud and rainfalls to emergencies
Of village skills and the aboriginal flash

Of handsome paddles among the bright rocks
And channels of the savage country.

• RETURN

This Earth the king said
Looking at the ground;
This England. But we drive
A Sunday paradise
Of parkway, trees flow into trees and the grass
Like water by the very asphalt crown
And summit of things
In the flow of traffic
The family cars, in the dim
Sound of the living
The noise of increase to which we owe
What we possess. We cannot reconcile ourselves.
No one is reconciled, tho we spring
From the ground together —

And we saw the seed,
The minuscule Sequoia seed
In the museum by the tremendous slab
Of the tree. And imagined the seed
In soil and the growth quickened
So that we saw the seed reach out, forcing
Earth thru itself into bark, wood, the green
Needles of a redwood until the tree
Stood in the room without soil —
How much of the earth's
Crust has lived
The seed's violence!
The shock is metaphysical.

For the wood weathers. Drift wood
And the foot print in the forest grow older.
This is not our time, not what we mean, it is a time
Passing, the curl at the cutwater,
The enormous prow
Outside in the weather. In that breeze,
The sense of that passage,
Is desertion,
Betrayal, that we are not innocent
Of loneliness as Pierrot, Pierrette chattering
Unaware tho we imagine nothing
Beyond the streets of the living —
A sap in the limbs. Mary,
Mary, we turn to the children
As they will turn to the children
Wanting so much to have created happiness
As if a stem to the leaves —

— we had camped in scrub,
A scrub of the past, the fringes of towns
Neither towns nor forest, nothing ours. And Linda five,
Maybe six when the mare grazing
In the meadow came to her.
'Horse,' she said, whispering
By the roadside
With the cars passing. Little girl welcomed,
Learning welcome. The rest is —

Whatever — whatever — remote
Mechanics, endurance,
The piers of the city
In the sea. Here are whole buildings

Razed, whole blocks
Of a city gone
Among old streets
And the old boroughs, ourselves
Among these streets where Petra beat
A washpan out her window gathering
A crowd like a rescue. Relief,
As they said it, The Relief. Petra
Decisive suddenly among her children
In those crumbling bedrooms, Petra,
Petra —. And how imagine it? or imagine
Coughlin in the streets,
Pelley and the Silver Shirts? The medieval sense seems
          innocent, the very
Ceremony of innocence that was drowned.
It was not. But how imagine it
Of streets boarded and vacant where no time will hatch
Now chairs and walls,
Floors, roofs, the joists and beams,
The woodwork, window sills
In sun in a great weight of brick.

• FROM DISASTER

Ultimately the air
Is bare sunlight where must be found
The lyric valuables. From disaster

Shipwreck, whole families crawled
To the tenements, and there

Survived by what morality
Of hope

Which for the sons
Ends its metaphysic
In small lawns of home.

• SARA IN HER FATHER'S ARMS

Cell by cell the baby made herself, the cells
Made cells. That is to say
The baby is made largely of milk. Lying in her father's arms,
        the little seed eyes
Moving, trying to see, smiling for us
To see, she will make a household
To her need of these rooms — Sara, little seed,
Little violent, diligent seed. Come let us look at the world
Glittering: this seed will speak,
Max, words! There will be no other words in the world
But those our children speak. What will she make of a world
Do you suppose, Max, of which she is made.

● BLOOD FROM THE STONE

I

In the door,
Long legged, tall,
A weight of bone and flesh to her —
      Her eyes catch —
Carrying bundles. O!
Everything I am is
Us. Come home.

II

The Thirties. And
A spectre

In every street,
In all inexplicable crowds, what they did then
Is still their lives.

As thirty in a group —
To Home Relief — the unemployed —
Within the city's intricacies
Are these lives. Belief?
What do we believe
To live with? Answer.
Not invent — just answer — all
That verse attempts.
That we can somehow add each to each other?

— Still our lives.

III

And war.

More than we felt or saw.
There is a simple ego in a lyric,
A strange one in war.
To a body anything can happen,
Like a brick. Too obvious to say.
But all horror came from it.

      The need
To see past every rock, wall, forest
Among so many, carrying in its frightful danger
The brick body as in one's hands.
And rounding the corner of some wall
Into a farm yard — France —
The smell of wood-smoke from the kitchen;
An overwhelming sense of joy!
Stops everything. More still than the water trickling among
      the cobbles.
In boots. Steel helmet. Monstrous. Standing
Shut by the silent walls.

IV

Fifty years
Sidereal time
Together, and among the others,
The bequeathed pavements, the inherited lit streets:
Among them we were lucky — strangest word.

The planet's
Time.
Blood from a stone, life
From a stone dead dam. Mother
Nature! because we find the others
Deserted like ourselves and therefore brothers. Yet

So we lived
And chose to live

These were our times.

● BIRTHPLACE: NEW ROCHELLE

Returning to that house
And the rounded rocks of childhood — They have lasted
      well.

A world of things.

An aging man,
The knuckles of my hand
So jointed! I am this?

                              The house
My father's once, and the ground. There is a color of his
      times
In the sun's light.

A generation's mark.
It intervenes. My child,
Not now a child, our child
Not altogether lone in a lone universe that suffers time
Like stones in sun. For we do not.

● MYSELF I SING

Me! he says, hand on his chest.
Actually, his shirt.
                    And there, perhaps,
The question.

Pioneers! But trailer people?
Wood box full of tools —
                    The most
American. A sort of
Shrinking
        in themselves. A
Less than adult: old.

A pocket knife,
A tool —
        And I
Here talking to the man?
                    The sky

That dawned along the road
And all I've been
Is not myself? I think myself
Is what I've seen and not myself

A man marooned
No longer looks for ships, imagines
Anything on the horizon. On the beach
The ocean ends in water. Finds a dune
And on the beach sits near it. Two.
He finds himself by two.

Or more.
'Incapable of contact
Save in incidents'
                    And yet at night
Their weight is part of mine.
For we are all housed now, all in our apartments,
The world untended to, unwatched.
And there is nothing left out there
As night falls, but the rocks

● STRANGER'S CHILD

Sparrow in the cobbled street,
Little sparrow round and sweet,
Chaucer's bird —

              or if a leaf
Sparkle among leaves, among the season's
Leaves —

        The sparrow's feet,
Feet of the sparrow's child touch
Naked rock.

• OZYMANDIAS

The five
Senses gone

To the one sense,
The sense of prominence

Produce an art
De luxe.

And down town
The absurd stone trimming of the building tops

Rectangular in dawn, the shopper's
Thin morning monument.

● DEBT

That 'part
Of consciousness
That works':

A virtue, then, a skill
Of benches and the shock

Of the press where an instant on the steel bed
The manufactured part —

New!
And imperfect. Not as perfect
As the die they made
Which was imperfect. Checked

To tolerance

Among the pin ups, notices, conversion charts,
And skills, so little said of it.

• PRODUCT

There is no beauty in New England like the boats.
Each itself, even the paint white
Dipping to each wave each time
At anchor, mast
And rigging tightly part of it
Fresh from the dry tools
And the dry New England hands.
The bow soars, finds the waves
The hull accepts. Once someone
Put a bowl afloat
And there for all to see, for all the children,
Even the New Englander
Was boatness. What I've seen
Is all I've found: myself.

● WORKMAN

Leaving the house each dawn I see the hawk
Flagrant over the driveway. In his claws
That dot, that comma
Is the broken animal: the dangling small beast knows
The burden that he is: he has touched
The hawk's drab feathers. But the carpenter's is a culture
Of fitting, of firm dimensions,
Of post and lintel. Quietly the roof lies
That the carpenter has finished. The sea birds circle
The beaches and cry in their own way,
The innumerable sea birds, their beaks and their wings
Over the beaches and the sea's glitter.

Beyond the Hudson's
Unimportant water lapping
In the dark against the city's shores
Are the small towns, remnants
Of forge and coal yard. The bird's voice in their streets
May not mean much: a bird the age of a child chirping
At curbs and curb gratings,
At barber shops and townsmen
Born of girls —
Of girls! Girls gave birth . . . But the interiors
Are the women's: curtained,
Lit, the fabric
To which the men return. Surely they imagine
Some task beyond the window glass
And the fabrics as if an eventual brother
In the fields were nourished by all this in country
Torn by the trucks where towns
And the flat boards of homes
Visibly move at sunrise and the trees
Carry quickly into daylight the excited birds.

● TOURIST EYE

This activity, beginning in the midst of men . . .

1

The lights that blaze and promise
Where are so many — What is offered

In the wall and nest of lights?
The land

Lacked center:
We must look to Lever Brothers

Based in a square block.
A thousand lives

Within that glass. What is the final meaning
Of extravagance? Why are the office

Buildings, storehouses of papers,
The centers of extravagance?

2

The solitary are obsessed.
Apartments furnish little solitude. Doors lock

On halls scarred
And painted. One might look everywhere

As tourists do, the halls and stairways
For something bequeathed

From time, some mark
In these most worn places

Where chance moves among the crowd
Unearned and separate

Among the crowd, the living, that other
Marvel among the mineral.

3

Rectangular, rearing
Black windows into daylight: the sound

Of a piano in the deep bulk tying
Generations to a Sunday that holds
As the building holds, only the adamant

Nothing that the child hopes,
Laboring a tune. From any window, the day

Flawless and without exterior
Without alternative. But to the tenant

The future is all chance, all future, and the present
All inanimate, or all herself.

4

The heart pounds
To be among them, the buildings,
The red buildings of Red Hook! In the currents of the harbor
The barn-red ferries on their curving courses
And the tides of Buttermilk Channel
Flow past the Brooklyn Hardware stores

And the homes
The aging homes
Of the workmen. This is a sense of order
And of threat. The essential city,
The necessary city
Among these harbor streets still visible.

5

Down-town
Swarms. Surely the oldest city,

It seems the oldest city in the world. Tho they are new in it.

                    But they too can become a fist
Having menace, the power of menace. After the headlines
        of last night

The streets appear unchanged,
Tho they are endangered,

By no means safe, the building tops
Unwarned and unwarnable.

• VULCAN

The householder issuing to the street
Is adrift a moment in that ice stiff
Exterior. 'Peninsula
Low lying in the bay
And wooded —' Native now
Are the welder and the welder's arc
In the subway's iron circuits:
We have not escaped each other,
Not in the forest, not here. The crippled girl hobbles
Painfully in the new depths
Of the subway, and painfully
We shift our eyes. The bare rails
And black walls contain
Labor before her birth, her twisted
Precarious birth and the men
Laborious, burly — She sits
Quiet, her eyes still. Slowly,
Deliberately she sees
An anchor's blunt fluke sink
Thru coins and coin machines,
The ancient iron and the voltage
In the iron beneath us in the child's deep
Harbors into harbor sand.

• FROM A PHOTOGRAPH

Her arms around me — child —
Around my head, hugging with her whole arms,
Whole arms as if I were a loved and native rock,
The apple in her hand — her apple and her father, and my
      nose pressed
Hugely to the collar of her winter coat. There in the photo-
      graph

It is the child who is the branch
We fall from, where would be bramble,
Brush, bramble in the young Winter
With its blowing snow she must have thought
Was ours to give to her.

• THE TUGS OF HULL

Carrying their deckhands' bicycles
On deck beside the funnels,
Coming alongside in falling snow
As we had moved thru areas of falling snow
In shrunk northern curvatures
Of seas that are not East nor West —. Was it there you told
        of the man and the water of the Ganges,
The man with the domestic pitcher pouring the Ganges
Back? We imagined the Ganges
The warm belly of a girl swelled
Like India under the slacks. One might think himself Adam
Of the edges of the polar mist until the small black tugs of
        England
Came to fetch us in.

• TIME OF THE MISSILE

I remember a square of New York's Hudson River glinting
      between warehouses.
Difficult to approach the water below the pier
Swirling, covered with oil the ship at the pier
A steel wall: tons in the water,

Width.
The hand for holding,
Legs for walking,
The eye *sees!* It floods in on us from here to Jersey tangled
      in the grey bright air!

Become the realm of nations.

My love, my love,
We are endangered
Totally at last. Look
Anywhere to the sight's limit: space
Which is viviparous:

Place of the mind
And eye. Which can destroy us,
Re-arrange itself, assert
Its own stone chain reaction.

[handwritten annotation:] (1) Producing living young, (2) germinating while still attached to the parent plant.

• THE MEN OF SHEEPSHEAD

Eric — we used to call him Eric —
And Charlie Weber: I knew them well,
Men of another century. And still at Sheepshead
If a man carries pliers
Or maul down these rambling piers he is a man who fetches
Power into the afternoon
                              Speaking of things

End-for-end, butted to each other,
Dove-tailed, tenoned, doweled — Who is not at home
Among these men? who make a home
Of half truth, rules of thumb
Of cam and lever and whose docks and piers
Extend into the sea so self-contained.

● ANTIQUE

Against the glass
Towers, the elaborate
Horned handle of a saw
Dates back

Beyond small harbors
Facing Europe. Ship's hawser
On the iron bollard at the land's edge mooring
Continents of workmen

Where we built
Grand Central's hollow masonry, veined
In bolted rails in shabby
City limits daylight and the back yard

Homes. In which some show of flowers
And of kitchen water holds survival's
Thin, thin radiance.

• COASTAL STRIP

The land runs in a flat strip of jungle along the coast.
A dirt road, mile after mile, passable
To trucks in the dry season crossing
Powerful rivers. Occasionally a truck
Stalls in mid stream, the men
In the current, the bright stream of the river laboring
Over the wet wheels, the washed tires —
Alien tons thru the jungle. One comes suddenly
On villages, groups of palm houses, the people
At ease before the palm branch homes. They speak
Casually, if the truck stops, for this is the road.
        There are towns,
Cement and stucco cities on the banks of the rivers,
People crowding the streets
Carrying machetes in the city squares. And the girls
Packed in a boat load, beautiful in their dresses, swirling
Downstream in the bright water
Crossing to the town. It has all
Already happened, there can be no breath
Of wind in the trees, the houses
Of earth and of palm from the jungle. *The sea that made us
        islands* has events
Of gulf and Gulf Stream and the gales
That move across it —. We have come from some powerful
Surf to the West where that sea breaks
In salt on the continent.

● O WESTERN WIND

A world around her like a shadow
She moves a chair
Something is being made —
Prepared
Clear in front of her as open air

The space a woman makes and fills
After these years
I write again
Naturally, about your face

Beautiful and wide
Blue eyes
Across all my vision but the glint of flesh
Blue eyes
In the subway routes, in the small rains
The profiles.

● THE HILLS

That this is I,
Not mine, which wakes
To where the present
Sun pours in the present, to the air perhaps
Of love and of
Conviction.

      As to know
Who we shall be. I knew it then.
You getting in
The old car sat down close
So close I turned and saw your eyes a woman's
Eyes. The patent
Latches on the windows
And the long hills whoever else's
Also ours.

● THE SOURCE

If the city has roots, they are in filth.
It is a slum. Even the sidewalk
Rasps under the feet.

       — In some black brick
       Tenement, a woman's body

Glows. The gleam; the unimaginable
Thin feet taper down
The instep naked to the wooden floor!

       Hidden and disguised
       — and shy?

The city's
Secret warmth.

• CHARTRES

The bulk of it
In air

Is what they wanted. Compassion
Above the doors, the doorways

Mary the woman and the others
The lesser

Are dreams on the structure. But that a stone
Supports another

That the stones
Stand where the masons locked them

Above the farmland
Above the will

Because a hundred generations
Back of them and to another people

The world cried out above the mountain

● THE CROWDED COUNTRIES OF THE BOMB

What man could do,
And could not
And chance which has spared us
Choice, which has shielded us

As if a god. What is the name of that place
We have entered:
Despair? Ourselves?

That we can destroy ourselves
Now

Walking in the shelter,
The young and the old,
Of each other's backs and shoulders

Entering the country that is
Impenetrably ours.

• DAEDALUS: THE DIRGE

The boy accepted them;
His whole childhood in them, his difference
From the others. The wings
Gold,
Gold for credence,
Every feather of them. He believed more in the things
Than I, and less. Familiar as speech,
The family tongue. I remember
Now expedients, frauds, ridiculous
In the real withering sun blazing
Still. Who could have said
More, losing the boy anyway, anyway
In the bare field there old man, old potterer . . .

• PART OF THE FOREST

There are lovers who recall that
Moment of moonlight, lit
Instant —

But to be alone is to be lost
Altho the tree, the roots
Are there

       It is an oak: the word
Terrifying spoken to the oak —

The young men therefore are determined to be men.
Beer bottle and a closed door
Makes them men.

Or car. — Approach
A town to be negotiated
By the big machine

Slow, for a young
Woman, kids
In hand. She is

A family. Isn't tenderness, God knows,
This long boned girl — it is a kind of war,
       A tower

In the suburb.

Then the road again. The car's
Companion.

● SURVIVAL: INFANTRY

And the world changed.
There had been trees and people,
Sidewalks and roads

There were fish in the sea.

Where did all the rocks come from?
And the smell of explosives
Iron standing in mud
We crawled everywhere on the ground without seeing the
      earth again

We were ashamed of our half life and our misery: we saw
      that everything had died.

And the letters came. People who addressed us thru our
      lives
They left us gasping. And in tears
In the same mud in the terrible ground

• SQUALL

      coming about
When the squall knocked her
Flat on the water. When she came
Upright, her rig was gone
And her crew clinging to her. The water in her cabins,
Washing thru companionways and hatches
And the deep ribs
Had in that mid-passage
No kinship with any sea.

The headland towers over ocean
At Palos Verdes. Who shall say
How the Romantic stood in nature?
But I am sitting in an automobile
While Mary, lovely in a house dress, buys tomatoes from a
      road side stand.

And I look down at the Pacific, blue waves roughly small
      running at the base of land,
An area of ocean in the sun —
Out there is China. Somewhere out in air.
Tree by the stand
Moving in the wind that moves
Streaming with the waves of the Pacific going past.

                   The beach: a child
Leaning on one elbow. She has swept an arm
To make a hollow and a mark around her in the sand,
A place swept smooth in one arm's claiming sweep beside
      the ocean,
Looking up the coast relaxed,
A Western child.
And all the air before her — what the wind brings past
In the bright simpleness and strangeness of the sands.

● SUNNYSIDE CHILD

As the builders
Planned, the city trees
Put leaves in summer air in lost
Streets above the subway. And in this

Achievement of the housed, this
Air, a child
Stands as a child,
Preoccupied

To find his generation, his contemporaries
Of the neighborhood whose atmosphere, whose sound
In his life's time no front door, no
Hardware ever again can close on.

● PEDESTRIAN

What generations could have dreamed
This grandchild of the shopping streets, her eyes

In the buyer's light, the store lights
Brighter than the lighthouses, brighter than moonrise

From the salt harbor so rich
So bright her city

In a soil of pavement, a mesh of wires where she walks
In the new winter among enormous buildings.

• TO MEMORY

(From a poem by Buddhadeva Bose)

I

Who but the Goddess? All that is
Is yours. The causes, beginnings,
Are lost if you have lost them;
But from your eyelid's quiver

Flowers that are trampled spring
In their bloom before us, and a landscape deepens
Hill behind hill, and the branches
Bend in that sunlight —

The lute has no meaning,
Nor canvas, nor marble
Without you, nor the beaches

That shore the ocean,
The womb of our mother. Galaxies
Shine in that darkness —

O you who are darkness,
A core of our darkness, and illumination;
What your hands have let fall is lost to us.

II

Words, there are words!
But with your eyes
We see. And so we possess the earth.

Like an army of ants,
A multiple dry carcass
Of past selves

Moving
Thru a land dead behind us
Of deeds, dates, documents

Into the present of leaves.
What can our changes bring
To the flesh but the worm's old feast?

All that there is, is
Yours, and in the caves of your sleep
Lives in our permanent dawn.

- STILL LIFE

(From a poem by Buddhadeva Bose)

What *are* you, apple! There are men
Who, biting an apple, blind themselves to bowl, basket
Or whatever and in a strange spell feel themselves
Like you outdoors and make us wish
We too were in the sun and night alive with sap.

• LEVIATHAN

Truth also is the pursuit of it:
Like happiness, and it will not stand.

Even the verse begins to eat away
In the acid. Pursuit, pursuit;

A wind moves a little,
Moving in a circle, very cold.

How shall we say?
In ordinary discourse —

We must talk now. I am no longer sure of the words,
The clockwork of the world. What is inexplicable

Is the 'preponderance of objects.' The sky lights
Daily with that predominance

And we have become the present.

We must talk now. Fear
Is fear. But we abandon one another.

- THIS IN WHICH

'Wait a minute,' Randall said insistently. 'Are you trying to describe the creation of the world—the universe?'

'What else?'

'But—damn it, this is preposterous! I asked for an explanation of the things that have just happened to *us*.'

'I told you that you would not like the explanation.'

> —Robert A. Heinlein, *The Unpleasant Profession of Jonathan Hoag*

'. . . the arduous path of appearance.'

> —Martin Heidegger

• TECHNOLOGIES

Tho in a sort of summer the hard buds blossom
Into feminine profusion

The 'inch-sized
Heart,' the little core of oneself,
So inartistic,

The inelegant heart
Which cannot grasp
The world
And makes art

Is small

Like a small hawk
Lighting disheveled on a window sill.

Like hawks we are at least not
Nowhere, and I would say
Where we are

Tho I distract
Windows that look out
On the business
Of the days

In streets
Without horizon, streets
And gardens

Of the feminine technologies
Of desire
And compassion which will clothe

Everyone, arriving
Out of uncivil
Air
Evil
As a hawk

From a hawk's
Nest as they say
The nest of such a bird

Must be, and continue
Therefore to talk about
Twig technologies

- ARMIES OF THE PLAIN

1

'A zero, a nothing':   *Oswald*
Assassin.

Not nothing. At nineteen
Crossing frontiers,

Rifleman of the suffering—
Irremediable suffering—of the not-great,

Hero and anti hero
Of our time

Despite all he has cost us
And he may have cost us very much

2

Ruby's day,
Bloomsday. —

Ruby

Proud to have learned survival
On the harsh plains — —

Bloomsday.

A man
'Of the Jewish faith . . .'

'and it is so stupid . .
And I never use the term . .'

Whose people wrote
Greatly

Desperate the not great,
Like Oswald the not great

Locked
In combat.

• PHILAI TE KOU PHILAI

There is a portrait by Eakins
Of the Intellectual, a man
Who might be a school teacher
Shown with the utmost seriousness, a masculine drama
In the hardness of his black shoes, in the glitter
Of his eyeglasses and his firm stance—
How have we altered! As Charles said
Rowing on the lake
In the woods, 'if this were the country,
The nation, if these were the routes through it—'

How firm the man is
In that picture
Tho pedagogic.
This was his world. Grass
Grows to the water's edge
In these woods, the brown earth
Shows through the thinned grass
At the little landing places of vacation

Like deserted stations,
Small embarkation points: We are
Lost in the childish
Here, and we address
Only each other
In the flat bottomed lake boat
Of boards. It is a lake
In a bend of the parkway, the breeze
Moves among the primitive toys
Of vacation, the circle of the visible

The animal looked across

And saw my eyes . . . Vacation's interlude?
When the animal ran? What entered the mind
When dawn lit the iron locomotives,
The iron bridges at the edge of the city,

Underpinnings, bare structure,
The animal's bare eyes

In the woods . . .
'The relation of the sun and the earth

Is not nothing! The sea in the morning'
And the hills brightening, Loved

And not loved, the unbearable impact
Of conviction and the beds of the defeated,

Children waking in the beds of the defeated
As the day breaks on the million

Windows and the grimed sills
Of a ruined ethic

Bursting with ourselves, and the myths
Have been murderous,

Most murderous, stake
And faggot. Where can it end? Loved, Loved

And Hated,
Rococo boulevards

Backed by the Roman
Whose fluted pillars

Blossoming antique acanthus

Stand on other coasts
Lifting their tremendous cornices.

• PSALM

Veritas sequitur . . .

In the small beauty of the forest
The wild deer bedding down—
That they are there!

           Their eyes
Effortless, the soft lips
Nuzzle and the alien small teeth
Tear at the grass

           The roots of it
Dangle from their mouths
Scattering earth in the strange woods.
They who are there.

           Their paths
Nibbled thru the fields, the leaves that shade them
Hang in the distances
Of sun

           The small nouns
Crying faith
In this in which the wild deer
Startle, and stare out.

These are the small resorts
Of the small poor,
The low sandspits
And the honkytonks
On the far side
Of the becalmed bay. The pennant
Flies from the flagstaff
Of the excursion steamer
Which carried us
In its old cabins
Crossing the bay
Tho it is flimsily built
And fantastic, its three white decks
Towering now above the pier
That extends from the beach
Into water barely deep enough
Over the sand bottom.

1

THE GESTURE

The question is: how does one hold an apple
Who likes apples

And how does one handle
Filth? The question is

How does one hold something
In the mind which he intends

To grasp and how does the salesman
Hold a bauble he intends

To sell? The question is
When will there not be a hundred

Poets who mistake that gesture
For a style.

THE LITTLE HOLE

The little hole in the eye
Williams called it, the little hole

Has exposed us naked
To the world

And will not close.

Blankly the world
Looks in

And we compose
Colors

And the sense

Of home
And there are those

In it so violent
And so alone

They cannot rest.

3

THAT LAND

Sing like a bird at the open
Sky, but no bird
Is a man—

Like the grip
Of the Roman hand
On his shoulder, the certainties

Of place
And of time

Held him, I think
With the pain and the casual horror
Of the iron and may have left
No hope of doubt

Whereas we have won doubt
From the iron itself

And hope in death. So that
If a man lived forever he would outlive
Hope. I imagine open sky

Over Gethsemane,
Surely it was this sky.

4

PAROUSIA

Impossible to doubt the world: it can be seen
And because it is irrevocable

It cannot be understood, and I believe that fact is lethal

And man may find his catastrophe,
His Millennium of obsession.

                                    air moving,
a stone on a stone,
something balanced momentarily, in time might the lion

Lie down in the forest, less fierce
And solitary

Than the world, the walls
Of whose future may stand forever.

5

FROM VIRGIL

I, says the buzzard,
I—

Mind

Has evolved
Too long

If 'life is a search
For advantage.'

'At whose behest

Does the mind think?' Art
Also is not good

For us
Unless like the fool

Persisting
In his folly

It may rescue us
As only the true

Might rescue us, gathered
In the smallest corners

Of man's triumph. *Parve puer* . . . 'Begin,

O small boy,
To be born;

On whom his parents have not smiled

No god thinks worthy of his table,
No goddess of her bed'

• THE FORMS OF LOVE

Parked in the fields
All night
So many years ago,
We saw
A lake beside us
When the moon rose.
I remember

Leaving that ancient car
Together. I remember
Standing in the white grass
Beside it. We groped
Our way together
Downhill in the bright
Incredible light

Beginning to wonder
Whether it could be lake
Or fog
We saw, our heads
Ringing under the stars we walked
To where it would have wet our feet
Had it been water

• GUEST ROOM

There is in age

The risk that the mind
Reach

Into homelessness, 'nowhere to return.' In age
The maxims

Expose themselves, the happy endings
That justify a moral. But this?

This? the noise of wealth,

The clamor of wealth—tree
So often shaken—it is the voice

Of Hell.
The virtue of the mind

Is that emotion

Which causes
To see. Virtue . . .

Virtue . . . ? The great house
With its servants,

The great utensiled
House

Of air conditioners, safe harbor

In which the heart sinks, closes
Now like a fortress

In daylight, setting its weight
Against the bare blank paper.

•   •

The purpose
Of their days.

And their nights?
Their evenings
And the candle light?

What could they mean by that?
Because the hard light dims

Outside, what ancient
Privilege? What gleaming
Mandate

From what past?

• •

If one has only his ability

To arrange
Matters, to exert force,

To open a window,
To shut it—

To cause to be arranged—

Death which is a question

Of an intestine
Or a sinus drip

Looms as the horror
Which will arrive

When one is most without defenses,

The unspeakable
Defeat

Toward which they live
Embattled and despairing;

It is the courage of the rich

Who are an *avant garde*

Near the limits of life—Like theirs

My abilities
Are ridiculous:

To go perhaps unarmed
And unarmored, to return

Now to the old questions—

●　　●

Of the dawn
Over Frisco
Lighting the large hills
And the very small coves
At their feet, and we
Perched in the dawn wind
Of that coast like leaves
Of the most recent weed—And yet the things

That happen! Signs,
Promises—we took it
As sign, as promise

Still for nothing wavered,
Nothing begged or was unreal, the thing
Happening, filling our eyesight
Out to the horizon—I remember the sky
And the moving sea.

- GIOVANNI'S *RAPE OF THE SABINE WOMEN*
  AT WILDENSTEIN'S

Showing the girl
On the shoulder of the warrior, calling

Behind her in the young body's triumph
With its despairing arms aloft

And the men violent,
being violent

In a strange village. The dust

Settles into village clarity
Among the villagers, a difficult

Song
Full of treason.

Sing?

To one's fellows?
To old men? in the villages,

The dwindling heritage
The heart will shrivel in

Sometime—But the statue!

Spiraling its drama
In the stair well

Of the gallery . . . Useless!
Useless! Thick witted,

Thick carpeted, exhilarated by the stylish
Or the opulent, the blind and deaf. There was the child

The girl was:

Seeking like a child the eyes
Of the animals

To promise
Everything that matters, shelter

From the winds

The winds that lie
In the mind,
The ruinous winds

'Powerless to affect
The intensity of what is'—

'It has been good to us,'
However. The nights

At sea, and what

We sailed in, the large
Loose sphere of it

Visible, the force in it
Moving the little boat.

Only that it changes! Perhaps one is himself
Beyond the heart, the center of the thing

And cannot praise it

As he would want to, with the light in it, feeling the long
        helplessness
Of those who will remain in it

And the losses. If this is treason
To the artists, make the most of it; one needs such faith,

Such faith in it
In the whole thing, more than I,
Or they, have had in songs.

1

A city of the corporations

Glassed
In dreams

And images—

And the pure joy
Of the mineral fact

Tho it is impenetrable

As the world, if it is matter

Is impenetrable.

2

Unable to begin
At the beginning, the fortunate
Find everything already here. They are shoppers,
Choosers, judges . . . And here the brutal
Is without issue, a dead end.

                              They develop
Argument in order to speak, they become
unreal, unreal, life loses
solidity, loses extent, baseball's their game
because baseball is not a game
but an argument and difference of opinion
makes the horse races. They are ghosts that endanger

One's soul. There is change
In an air
That smells stale, they will come to the end
Of an era
First of all peoples
And one may honorably keep
His distance
If he can.

3

I cannot even now
Altogether disengage myself
From those men

With whom I stood in emplacements, in mess tents,
In hospitals and sheds and hid in the gullies
Of blasted roads in a ruined country,

Among them many men
More capable than I—

Muykut and a sergeant
Named Healy,
That lieutenant also—

How forget that? How talk
Distantly of 'the People'?

Who are the people? that they are

That force within the walls
Of cities

Wherein the cars
Of mechanics
And executives

Echo like history
Down walled avenues
In which one cannot speak.

4

Possible
To use
Words provided one treat them
As enemies.
Not enemies—Ghosts
Which have run mad
In the subways
And of course the institutions
And the banks. If one captures them
One by one proceeding

Carefully they will restore
I hope to meaning
And to sense.

5

Which act is
Violence

And no one makes do with a future
Of rapid travel with diminishing noise
Less jolting
And fewer drafts. They await

War, and the news
Is war
As always

That the juices may flow in them
And the juices lie.

Great things have happened
On the earth and given it history, armies
And the ragged hordes moving and the passions
Of that death

But who escapes
Death?

Whether or not there is war, whether he has
Or has not opinions, and not only warriors,
Not only heroes

And not only victims, and they may have come to the end
Of all that, and if they have
They may have come to the end of it.

6

There can be a brick
In a brick wall
The eye picks

So quiet of a Sunday.
Here is the brick, it was waiting
Here when you were born,

Mary-Anne

7

Strange that the youngest people I know
Like Mary-Anne live in the most ancient buildings

Scattered about the city
In the dark rooms
Of the past—and the immigrants,

The black
Rectangular buildings
Of the immigrants.

They are the children of the middle class.

'The pure products of America—'

Investing
The ancient buildings
Jostle each other

In the half-forgotten, that ponderous business,
This Chinese wall.

8

Whitman: 'April 19, 1864

The capital grows upon one in time, especially as they have got the great figure on top of it now, and you can see it very well. It is a great bronze figure, the Genius of Liberty I suppose. It looks wonderful toward sundown. I love to go and look at it. The sun when it is nearly down shines on the headpiece and it dazzles and glistens like a big star; it looks quite

curious . . .'

- EROS   *Paris*

Show me also whether there is more to come than is past,
or the greater part has already gone by us.—Second Esdras

'and you too, old man, so we have heard,
Once . . .'
An old man's head, bulging
And worn

Almost into death.

The head grows from within
And is eroded.

Yet they come here too, the old,
Among the visitors, suffering
The rain

Here above Paris—

To the plaque of the ten thousand
Last men of the Commune
Shot at that wall

In the cemetery of Père-Lachaise, and the grave
Of Largo Caballero and the monuments to the Resistance—

A devoutness

Toward the future
Recorded in this city
Which taught my generation

Art
And the great paved places
Of the cities.

Maze

And wealth
Of heavy ancestry and the foreign rooms

Of structures

Closed by their roofs
And complete, a culture

Mined
From the ground . . .

As tho the powerful gift
Of their presence
And the great squares void
Of their dead

Were the human tongue
That will speak.

• BOY'S ROOM

A friend saw the rooms
Of Keats and Shelley
At the lake, and saw 'they were just
Boys' rooms' and was moved

By that. And indeed a poet's room
Is a boy's room
And I suppose that women know it.

Perhaps the unbeautiful banker
Is exciting to a woman, a man
Not a boy gasping
For breath over a girl's body.

● PENOBSCOT   *New England*

Children of the early
Countryside

Talk on the back stoops
Of that locked room
Of their birth

Which they cannot remember

In these small stony worlds
In the ocean

Like a core
Of an antiquity

Non classic, anti-classic, not the ocean
But the flat
Water of the harbor
Touching the stone

They stood on—

I think we will not breach the world
These small worlds least
Of all with secret names

Or unexpected phrases—

Penobscot

Half deserted, has an air
Of northern age, the rocks and pines

And the inlets of the sea
Shining among the islands

And these innocent
People
In their carpentered

Homes, nailed
Against the weather—It is more primitive

Than I know
To live like this, to tinker
And to sleep

Near the birches
That shine in the moonlight

Distant
From the classic world—the north

Looks out from its rock
Bulging into the fields, wild flowers
Growing at its edges! It is a place its women

Love, which is the country's
Distinction—

The canoes in the forest
And the small prows of the fish boats
Off the coast in the dead of winter

That burns like a Tyger
In the night sky. One sees their homes and lawns,
The pale wood houses

And the pale green
Terraced lawns.
'It brightens up into the branches

And against the buildings'
Early. That was earlier.

• SEATED MAN

The man is old and—
Out of scale

Sitting in the rank grass. The fact is
It is not his world. Tho it holds

The machine which has so long sustained him,
The plumbing, sidewalks, the roads

And the objects
He has owned and remembers.
He thinks of murders and torture

In the German cellars
And the resistance of heroes

Picturing the concrete walls.

- STREET

Ah these are the poor,
These are the poor—

Bergen street.

Humiliation,
Hardship . . .

Nor are they very good to each other;
It is not that. I want

An end of poverty
As much as anyone

For the sake of intelligence,
'The conquest of existence'—

It has been said, and is true—

And this is real pain,
Moreover. It is terrible to see the children,

The righteous little girls;
So good, they expect to be so good . . ..

• CARPENTER'S BOAT

The new wood as old as carpentry

Rounding the far buoy, wild
Steel fighting in the sea, carpenter,

Carpenter,
Carpenter and other things, the monstrous welded seams

Plunge and drip in the seas, carpenter,
Carpenter, how wild the planet is.

There are the feminine aspects,
The mode in which one lives
As tho the color of the air
Indoors
And not indoors

Only—. What distinction
I have is that I have lived
My adult life
With a beautiful woman, I have turned on the light
Sometimes, to see her

Sleeping—The girl who walked
Indian style—straight-toed—
With her blond hair
Thru the forests

Of Oregon
Has changed the aspect
Of things, everything is pierced
By her presence tho we have wanted
Not comforts

But vision
Whatever terrors
May have made us
Companion
To the earth, whatever terrors—

For love we all go
To that mountain
Of human flesh
Which exists
And is incapable
Of love and which we saw
In the image
Of a woman—We said once
She was beautiful for she was
Suffering
And beautiful. She was more ambitious
Than we knew
Of wealth
And more ruthless—speaking
Still in that image—we will never be free
Again from the knowledge
Of that hatred
And that huge contempt. Will she not rot
Without us and die
In childbed leaving
Monstrous issue—

• BAHAMAS

Where are we,
Mary, where are we?
They screen us and themselves
With tree lined lanes

And the gardens of hotels tho we have traveled
Into the affluent tropics. The harbors
Pierce all that. There are these islands

Breaking the surface
Of the sea. They are the sandy peaks
Of hills in an ocean

Streaked green by their shoals. The fishermen
And the crews from Haiti
Tide their wooden boats out

In the harbors. Not even the guitarists
Singing the island songs
To the diners

Tell of the Haitian boats
Which bear their masts, the tall
Stripped trunks of trees

(Perhaps a child
Barefoot on the ragged deck-load
Of coconuts and mats, leans

On the worn mast) across the miles
Of the Atlantic, and the blinding glitter
Of the sea.

• THE FOUNDER

Because he could not face
A whole day
From dawn

He lay late
As the privileged
Lie in bed.

Yet here as he planned
Is his village
Enduring

The astronomic light
That wakes a people
In the painful dawn.

• PRIMITIVE

A woman dreamed
In that *jacal,* a jungle hut, and awoke
Screaming in terror. The hut
Stands where the beach
Curves to a bay. Here the dug-out is hauled
Clear of the surf, and she awoke
In fear. Their possessions
Are in the hut and around it
On the clean ground under the trees: a length
       of palm trunk
Roughened by uses, a wash tub,
The delicate fish lines
His fingers know so well—
They were visible in the clear night. Here she awoke

Crying in nightmare
Of loss, calling her husband
And the baby woke also
Crying

• ALPINE

We were hiding
Somewhere in the Alps
In a barn among animals. We knew
Our daughter should not know
We were there. It was cold
Was the point of the dream
And the snow was falling

Which must be an old dream of families
Dispersing into adulthood

And the will cowers
In the given

The outlaw winds
That move within barns

Intolerable breeze
A public music

Seeps thru the legendary walls
The cracked inner sides

The distinctions of what one does
And what is done to him blurrs

Bodies dream selves
For themselves

From the substance
Of the cold

Yet we move
Are moving

Are we not

Do we hear the heavy moving
Of the past in barns

- RATIONALITY

   there is no 'cure'
Of it, a reversal
Of some wrong decision—merely

The length of time that has passed
And the accumulation of knowledge.

To say again: the massive heart
Of the present, the presence
Of the machine tools

In the factories, and the young workman
Elated among the men
Is homesick

In that instant
Of the shock
Of the press

In which the manufactured part

New in its oil
On the steel bed is caught
In the obstinate links

Of cause, like the earth tilting
To its famous Summers—that 'part

of consciousness'. . .

• NIGHT SCENE

The drunken man
On an old pier
In the Hudson River,

Tightening his throat, thrust his chin
Forward and the light
Caught his raised face,
His eyes still blind with drink . . .

Said, to my wife
And to me—
He must have been saying

Again—

Good bye Momma,
Good bye Poppa

On an old pier.

• THE MAYAN GROUND

. . . and whether they are beautiful or not there will be
no one to guard them in the days to come . .

We mourned the red cardinal birds and the jeweled
    ornaments
And the handful of precious stones in our fields . . .

Poor savages
Of ghost and glitter. Merely rolling now

The tire leaves a mark
On the earth, a ridge in the ground

Crumbling at the edges
Which is terror, the unsightly

Silting sand of events—

Inside that shell, 'the speckled egg'
The poet wrote of that we try to break

Each day, the little grain,

Electron, beating
Without cause,

Dry grain, father

Of all our fathers
Hidden in the blazing shell

Of sunlight—. Savages,

Savages, there is no mystery about them,
Given the rest of it,

They who have evolved
In it, and no one to shield them

Therefore in the days to come, in the ruts
Of the road

Or the fields, or the thin
Air of the berserk mountains—. But the god!

They said,
Moving on the waters,

The breeze on the water, feathery
Serpent,

Wind on the surface,
On the shallows

And the count of the calendar had become confused.

They said they had lost account
Of the *unrolling of the universe*

And only the people

Stir in the mornings
Coming from the houses, and the black hair

Of the women at the pump

Against the dawn
Seems beautiful.

Note: Italicized phrases are quoted from *The Book of the Jaguar Priest; A translation of the book of Chilam Balam of Tizimin* by Maud Worcester Makemson (New York, Henry Schuman, 1951).

• QUOTATIONS

1

When I asked the very old man
In the Bahamas
How old the village was
He said,
'I found it.'

2

The infants and the animals
And the insects
'stare at the open'

And she said
Therefore they are welcome.

3

'. . . and her closets!
No real clothes—just astounding earrings
And perfumes and bright scarves and dress-up things—

She said she was "afraid," she said she was
"always afraid." '

4

And the child
We took on a trip
Said

'We're having the life of our times'

5

Someone has scrawled
Under an advertisement in the subway
Showing a brassy blond young woman
With an elaborate head-dress:
'Cop's bitch.'

(New York, 1962)

• RED HOOK: DECEMBER

We had not expected it, the whole street
Lit with the red, blue, green
And yellow of the Christmas lights
In the windows shining and blinking
Into distance down the cross streets.
The children are almost awed in the street
Putting out the trash paper
In the winking light. A man works
Patiently in his overcoat
With the little bulbs
Because the window is open
In December. The bells ring,

Ring electronically the New Year
Among the roofs
And one can be at peace
In this city on a shore
For the moment now
With wealth, the shining wealth.

• THE BICYCLES AND THE APEX

How we loved them
Once, these mechanisms;
We all did. Light
And miraculous,

They have gone stale, part
Of the platitude, the gadgets,
Part of the platitude
Of our discontent.

Van Gogh went hungry and what shoe salesman
Does not envy him now? Let us agree
Once and for all that neither the slums
Nor the tract houses

Represent the apex
Of the culture.
They are the barracks. Food

Produced, garbage disposed of,
Lotions sold, flat tires
Changed and tellers must handle money

Under supervision but it is a credit to no one
So that slums are made dangerous by the gangs
And suburbs by the John Birch Societies

But we loved them once,
The mechanisms. Light
And miraculous . . .

• THE OCCURRENCES

The simplest
Words say the grass blade
Hides the blaze
Of a sun
To throw a shadow
In which the bugs crawl
At the roots of the grass;

Father, father
Of fatherhood
Who haunts me, shivering
Man most naked
Of us all, O father

       watch
At the roots
Of the grass the creating
Now   that tremendous
plunge

• MONUMENT

Public silence indeed is nothing

So we confront the fact with stage craft
And the available poses

Of greatness,

One comes to the Norman chapel,
The Norman wall
Of the armed man
At the root of the thing,
Roughly armed,
The great sword, the great shield
And the helmet,
The horned helmet

On the mount
In the sea threatening
Its distances.

I was born to
A minor courage
And the harbor
We lived near, and the ungainliness
Of the merchants, my grandparents;

Of which I chose the harbor
And the sea

Which is a home and the homeless,
It is the sea,
Contrary of monuments
And illiberal.

• FLIGHT

Outside the porthole life, or what is
Not life streams in the air foils
Battering the wing tips, the houses
Small as in the skulls of birds, the frivolous ground

Of homes from which the force of motors
And the great riveted surfaces
Of the wings hold us, seated side by side
In flight, in the belly of force

Under the ceiling lights—the shabby bird
Of war, fear
And remoteness haunt it. We had made out
A highway, a city hall,

A park, but now the pastless ranches
Of the suburbs
Drift with the New World
Hills and the high regions

Which taken unaware
Resist, and the wings
Bend

In the open. Risk
And chance and event, pale
Ancestry beyond the portholes
Outside with the wings and the rivets.

• NIECE

The streets of San Francisco,
She said of herself, were my

Father and mother, speaking to the quiet guests
In the living room looking down the hills

To the bay. And we imagined her
Walking in the wooden past
Of the western city . . . her mother

Was not that city
But my elder sister. I remembered

The watchman at the beach
Telling us the war had ended—

That was the first world war
Half a century ago—my sister
Had a ribbon in her hair.

• THE ZULU GIRL

Her breasts
Naked, the soft
Small hollow in the flesh
Near the arm pit, the tendons
Presenting the gentle breasts
So boldly, tipped

With her intimate
Nerves

That touched, would touch her
Deeply—she stands
In the wild grasses.

• THE BUILDING OF THE SKYSCRAPER

The steel worker on the girder
Learned not to look down, and does his work
And there are words we have learned
Not to look at,
Not to look for substance
Below them. But we are on the verge
Of vertigo.

There are words that mean nothing
But there is something to mean.
Not a declaration which is truth
But a thing
Which is. It is the business of the poet
'To suffer the things of the world
And to speak them and himself out.'

O, the tree, growing from the sidewalk—
It has a little life, sprouting
Little green buds
Into the culture of the streets.
We look back
Three hundred years and see bare land.
And suffer vertigo.

• A NARRATIVE

1

I am the father of no country
And can lie.

But whether mendacity
Is really the best policy. And whether

One is not afraid
To lie.

2

And truth? O,
Truth!

Attack
On the innocent

If all we have
Is time.

3

The constant singing
Of the radios, and the art

Of colored lights
And the perfumist

Are also art. But here

Parallel lines do not meet
And the compass does not spin, this is the interval

In which they do not, and events
Emerge on the bow like an island, mussels

Clinging to its rocks from which kelp

Grows, grass
And the small trees

Above the tide line
And its lighthouse

Showing its whitewash in the daylight

In which things explain each other,
Not themselves.

4

An enclave
Filled with their own
Lives, they said, but they disperse

Into their jobs,
Their 'circles,' lose connection
With themselves . . . How shall they know

Themselves, bony
With age?
This is our home, the planets

Move in it
Or seem to,
It is our home. Wolves may hunt

With wolves, but we will lose
Humanity in the cities
And the suburbs, stores

And offices
In simple
Enterprise.

5

It is a place.
Nothing has entered it.
Nothing has left it.
People are born

From those who are there. How have I forgotten . .

How have we forgotten
That which is clear, we
Dwindle, but that I have forgotten
Tortures me.

6

I saw from the bus,
Walked in fact from the bus station to see again
The river and its rough machinery
On the sloping bank—I cannot know

Whether the weight of cause
Is in such a place as that, tho the depth of water
Pours and pours past Albany
From all its sources.

7

Serpent, Ouroboros
Whose tail is in his mouth: he is the root
Of evil,
This ring worm, the devil's
Doctrine the blind man
Knew. His mind
Is its own place;
He has no story. Digested

And digesting—Fool object,
Dingy medallion
In the gutter
Of Atlantic Avenue!
Let it alone! It is deadly.
What breath there is
In the rib cage we must draw
From the dimensions

Surrounding, whether or not we are lost
And choke on words.

8

But at night the park
She said, is horrible. And Bronk said
Perhaps the world
Is horror.
She did not understand. He meant
The waves or pellets
Are thrown from the process
Of the suns and like radar
Bounce where they strike. The eye
It happens
Registers
But it is dark.
It is the nature
Of the world:
It is as dark as radar.

9

      The lights
Shine, the fire
Glows in the fallacy
Of words. And one may cherish
Invention and the invented terms
We act on. But the park
Or the river at night
She said again
Is horrible.

10

Some of the young men
Have become aware of the Indian,
Perhaps because the young men move across the continent
Without wealth, moving one could say
On the bare ground. There one finds the Indian

Otherwise not found. Wood here and there
To make a village, a fish trap in a river,
The land pretty much as it was.

And because they also were a people in danger,
Because they feared also the thing might end,
I think of the Indian songs . . .
'There was no question what the old men were singing'
The anthropologist wrote,

Aware that the old men sang
On those prairies,
Return, the return of the sun.

11

River of our substance
Flowing
With the rest. River of the substance
Of the earth's curve, river of the substance
Of the sunrise, river of silt, of erosion, flowing
To no imaginable sea. But the mind rises

Into happiness, rising

Into what is there. I know of no other happiness
Nor have I ever witnessed it. . . . Islands
To the north

In polar mist
In the rather shallow sea—
Nothing more

But the sense
Of where we are

Who are most northerly. The marvel of the wave
Even here is its noise seething
In the world; I thought that even if there were nothing

The possibility of being would exist;
I thought I had encountered

Permanence; thought leaped on us in that sea
For in that sea we breathe the open
Miracle

Of place, and speak
If we would rescue
Love to the ice-lit

Upper World a substantial language
Of clarity, and of respect.

• PRO NOBIS

I believe my apprenticeship
In that it was long was honorable
Tho I had hoped to arrive
At an actuality
In the mere number of us
And record now
That I did not.

Therefore pray for us
In the hour of our death indeed.

• TO C. T.

(Written originally in a letter to Charles Tomlinson who, in his reply, suggested this division into lines of verse. The poem is, therefore, a collaboration.)

One imagines himself
addressing his peers
I suppose. Surely
that might be the definition
of 'seriousness'? I would like,
as you see,
to convince
myself
that my pleasure in your response
is not
plain vanity
but the pleasure of being heard,
the pleasure
of companionship, which seems
more honorable.

• WORLD, WORLD—

Failure, worse failure, nothing seen
From prominence,
Too much seen in the ditch.

Those who will not look
Tho they feel on their skins
Are not pierced;

One cannot count them
Tho they are present.

It is entirely wild, wildest
Where there is traffic
And populace.

'Thought leaps on us' because we are here. That is the fact
        of the matter.
Soul-searchings, these prescriptions,

Are a medical faddism, an attempt to escape,
To lose oneself in the self.

The self is no mystery, the mystery is
That there is something for us to stand on.

We want to be here.

The act of being, the act of being
More than oneself.

- OF BEING NUMEROUS

1

There are things
We live among 'and to see them
Is to know ourselves'.

Occurrence, a part
Of an infinite series,

The sad marvels;

Of this was told
A tale of our wickedness.
It is not our wickedness.

'You remember that old town we went to, and we sat in the
ruined window, and we tried to imagine that we belonged to
those times—It is dead and it is not dead, and you cannot
imagine either its life or its death; the earth speaks and the
salamander speaks, the Spring comes and only obscures it—'

2

So spoke of the existence of things,
An unmanageable pantheon

Absolute, but they say
Arid.

A city of the corporations

Glassed
In dreams

And images—

And the pure joy
Of the mineral fact

Tho it is impenetrable

As the world, if it is matter,
Is impenetrable.

3

The emotions are engaged
Entering the city
As entering any city.

We are not coeval
With a locality
But we imagine others are,

We encounter them. Actually
A populace flows
Thru the city.

This is a language, therefore, of New York

4

For the people of that flow
Are new, the old

New to age as the young
To youth

And to their dwelling
For which the tarred roofs

And the stoops and doors—
A world of stoops—
Are petty alibi and satirical wit
Will not serve.

5

The great stone
Above the river
In the pylon of the bridge

'1875'

Frozen in the moonlight
In the frozen air over the footpath, consciousness

Which has nothing to gain, which awaits nothing,
Which loves itself

6

We are pressed, pressed on each other,
We will be told at once
Of anything that happens

And the discovery of fact bursts
In a paroxysm of emotion
Now as always.   Crusoe

We say was
'Rescued'.
So we have chosen.

7 *Conform.*

Obsessed, bewildered

By the shipwreck
Of the singular

We have chosen the meaning
Of being numerous.

8

Amor fati
The love of fate

For which the city alone
Is audience

Perhaps blasphemous.

Slowly over islands, destinies
Moving steadily pass
And change

In the thin sky
Over islands

Among days

Having only the force
Of days

Most simple
Most difficult

9

'Whether, as the intensity of seeing increases, one's distance
        from Them, the people, does not also increase'
I know, of course I know, I can enter no other place

Yet I am one of those who from nothing but man's way of
        thought and one of his dialects and what has happened
        to me
Have made poetry

To dream of that beach
For the sake of an instant in the eyes,

The absolute singular

The unearthly bonds
Of the singular

Which is the bright light of shipwreck

10

Or, in that light, New arts! Dithyrambic, audience-as-artists!
But I will listen to a man, I will listen to a man, and when I
speak I will speak, tho he will fail and I will fail. But I will
listen to him speak. The shuffling of a crowd is nothing—
well, nothing but the many that we are, but nothing.

Urban art, art of the cities, art of the young in the cities—
The isolated man is dead, his world around him exhausted

And he fails! He fails, that meditative man! And indeed they
cannot 'bear' it.

11

           it is *that* light
Seeps anywhere, a light for the times

In which the buildings
Stand on low ground, their pediments
Just above the harbor

Absolutely immobile,

Hollow, available, you could enter any building,
You could look from any window
One might wave to himself
From the top of the Empire State Building—

Speak

If you can

Speak

Phyllis—not neo-classic,
The girl's name is Phyllis—

Coming home from her first job
On the bus in the bare civic interior
Among those people, the small doors
Opening on the night at the curb
Her heart, she told me, suddenly tight with happiness—

So small a picture,
A spot of light on the curb, it cannot demean us

I too am in love down there with the streets
And the square slabs of pavement—

To talk of the house and the neighborhood and the docks

And it is not 'art'

12

'In these explanations it is presumed that an experiencing
subject is one occasion of a sensitive reaction to an actual
world.'

the rain falls
that had not been falling
and it is the same world

. . .

They made small objects
Of wood and the bones of fish
And of stone. They talked,
Families talked,
They gathered in council
And spoke, carrying objects.
They were credulous,
Their things shone in the forest.

They were patient
With the world.
This will never return, never,
Unless having reached their limits

They will begin over, that is,
Over and over

        unable to begin
At the beginning, the fortunate
Find everything already here. They are shoppers,
Choosers, judges; . . . And here the brutal
is without issue, a dead end.

                      They develop
Argument in order to speak, they become
unreal, unreal, life loses
solidity, loses extent, baseball's their game
because baseball is not a game
but an argument and difference of opinion
makes the horse races. They are ghosts that endanger

One's soul. There is change
In an air
That smells stale, they will come to the end
Of an era
First of all peoples
And one may honorably keep

His distance
If he can.

14

I cannot even now
Altogether disengage myself
From those men

With whom I stood in emplacements, in mess tents,
In hospitals and sheds and hid in the gullies
Of blasted roads in a ruined country,

Among them many men
More capable than I—

Muykut and a sergeant
Named Healy,
That lieutenant also—

How forget that? How talk
Distantly of 'The People'

Who are that force
Within the walls
Of cities

Wherein their cars

Echo like history
Down walled avenues
In which one cannot speak.

15

Chorus (androgynous): 'Find me
So that I will exist, find my navel
So that it will exist, find my nipples
So that they will exist, find every hair
Of my belly, I am good (or I am bad),
Find me.'

16

'. . . he who will not work shall not eat,
and only he who was troubled shall find rest,
and only he who descends into the nether world shall
        rescue his beloved,
and only he who unsheathes his knife shall be given
        Isaac again. He who will not work shall not eat . . .
but he who will work shall give birth to his own father.'

17

The roots of words
Dim in the subways

There is madness in the number
Of the living
'A state of matter'

There is nobody here but us chickens

Anti-ontology— *theories of existence*

He wants to say
His life is real,
No one can say why

It is not easy to speak

A ferocious mumbling, in public
Of rootless speech

18

It is the air of atrocity,
An event as ordinary
As a President.

A plume of smoke, visible at a distance
In which people burn.

19

Now in the helicopters the casual will
Is atrocious

Insanity in high places,
If it is true we must do these things
We must cut our throats

The fly in the bottle

Insane, the insane fly

Which, over the city
Is the bright light of shipwreck

20

—They await

War, and the news
Is war

As always

That the juices may flow in them
Tho the juices lie.

Great things have happened
On the earth and given it history, armies
And the ragged hordes moving and the passions
Of that death. But who escapes
Death

Among these riders
Of the subway,

They know
By now as I know

Failure and the guilt
Of failure.
As in Hardy's poem of Christmas

We might half-hope to find the animals
In the sheds of a nation
Kneeling at midnight,

Farm animals,
Draft animals, beasts for slaughter
Because it would mean they have forgiven us,
Or which is the same thing,
That we do not altogether matter.

21

There can be a brick
In a brick wall
The eye picks

So quiet of a Sunday
Here is the brick, it was waiting
Here when you were born

Mary-Anne.

22

Clarity

In the sense of *transparence,*
I don't mean that much can be explained.

Clarity in the sense of silence.

23

'Half free
And half mad'
And the jet set is in.
The vocabularies of the forties
Gave way to the JetStream
And the media, the Mustang
And the deals
And the people will change again.

Under the soil
In the blind pressure
The lump,
Entity
Of substance
Changes also.

In two dozen rooms,
Two dozen apartments
After the party
The girls
Stare at the ceilings
Blindly as they are filled
And then they sleep.

24

In this nation
Which is in some sense
Our home. Covenant!

The covenant is:
There shall be peoples.

25

Strange that the youngest people I know
Live in the oldest buildings

Scattered about the city
In the dark rooms
Of the past—and the immigrants,

The black
Rectangular buildings
Of the immigrants.

They are the children of the middle class.

'The pure products of America—'

Investing
The ancient buildings
Jostle each other

In the half-forgotten, that ponderous business.
This Chinese Wall.

26

They carry nativeness
To a conclusion
In suicide.

We want to defend
Limitation
And do not know how.

Stupid to say merely
That poets should not lead their lives
Among poets,

They have lost the metaphysical sense
Of the future, they feel themselves
The end of a chain

Of lives, single lives
And we know that lives
Are single

And cannot defend
The metaphysic
On which rest

The boundaries
Of our distances.
We want to say

'Common sense'
And cannot. We stand on

That denial
Of death that paved the cities,
Paved the cities

Generation
For generation and the pavement

Is filthy as the corridors
Of the police.

How shall one know a generation, a new generation?
Not by the dew on them! Where the earth is most torn
And the wounds untended and the voices confused,
There is the head of the moving column

Who if they cannot find
Their generation
Wither in the infirmaries

And the supply depots, supplying
Irrelevant objects.

Street lamps shine on the parked cars
Steadily in the clear night

It is true the great mineral silence
Vibrates, hums, a process
Completing itself

In which the windshield wipers
Of the cars are visible.

The power of the mind, the
Power and weight
Of the mind which
Is not enough, it is nothing
And does nothing

Against the natural world,
Behemoth, white whale, beast
They will say and less than beast,
The fatal rock

Which is the world—

O if the streets
Seem bright enough,
Fold within fold
Of residence . . .

Or see thru water
Clearly the pebbles
Of the beach
Thru the water, flowing
From the ripple, clear
As ever they have been

27

It is difficult now to speak of poetry—

about those who have recognized the range of choice or those
who have lived within the life they were born to—. It is not
precisely a question of profundity but a different order of
experience. One would have to tell what happens in a life,
what choices present themselves, what the world is for us,
what happens in time, what thought is in the course of a life
and therefore what art is, and the isolation of the actual

I would want to talk of rooms and of what they look out on
and of basements, the rough walls bearing the marks of the
forms, the old marks of wood in the concrete, such solitude
as we know—

and the swept floors. Someone, a workman bearing about
him, feeling about him that peculiar word like a dishonored
fatherhood has swept this solitary floor, this profoundly hid-
den floor—such solitude as we know.

One must not come to feel that he has a thousand threads
          in his hands,
He must somehow see the one thing;
This is the level of art
There are other levels
But there is no other level of art

28

The light
Of the closed pages, tightly closed, packed against each other
Exposes the new day,

The narrow, frightening light
Before a sunrise.

29

My daughter, my daughter, what can I say
Of living?

I cannot judge it.

We seem caught
In reality together my lovely
Daughter,

I have a daughter
But no child

And it was not precisely
Happiness we promised
Ourselves;

We say happiness, happiness and are not
Satisfied.

Tho the house on the low land
Of the city

Catches the dawn light

I can tell myself, and I tell myself
Only what we all believe
True

And in the sudden vacuum
Of time . . .

. . . is it not
In fear the roots grip

Downward
And beget

The baffling hierarchies
Of father and child

As of leaves on their high
Thin twigs to shield us

From time, from open
Time

30

Behind their house, behind the back porch
Are the little woods.
She walks into them sometimes
And awaits the birds and the deer.

Looking up she sees the blue bright sky
Above the branches.
If one had been born here
How could one believe it?

31

Because the known and the unknown
Touch,

One witnesses—.
It is ennobling
If one thinks so.

If to know is noble

It is ennobling.

32

Only that it should be beautiful,
Only that it should be beautiful,

O, beautiful

Red green blue—the wet lips
Laughing

Or the curl of the white shell

And the beauty of women, the perfect tendons
Under the skin, the perfect life

That can twist in a flood
Of desire

Not truth but each other

The bright, bright skin, her hands wavering
In her incredible need

33

Which is ours, which is ourselves,
This is our jubilation
Exalted and as old as that truthfulness
Which illumines speech.

34

Like the wind in the trees and the bells
Of the procession—

How light the air is
And the earth,

Children and the grass
In the wind and the voices of men and women

To be carried about the sun forever

Among the beautiful particulars of the breezes
The papers blown about the sidewalks

'. . . . a Female Will to hide the most evident God
Under a covert . . .'

Surely infiniteness is the most evident thing in the world

Is it the courage of women
To assume every burden of blindness themselves

Intruders
Carrying life, the young women

Carrying life
Unaided in their arms

In the streets, weakened by too much need
Of too little

And life seeming to depend on women, burdened and
          desperate
As they are

• 174

35

. . . or define
Man beyond rescue
of the impoverished, solve
whole cities

before we can face
again
forests and prairies . . .

36

Tho the world
Is the obvious, the seen
And unforeseeable,
That which one cannot
Not see

Which the first eyes
Saw—

For us
Also each
Man or woman
Near is
Knowledge

Tho it may be of the noon's
Own vacuity

—and the mad, too, speak only of conspiracy
and people talking—

And if those paths
Of the mind
Cannot break

It is not the wild glare
Of the world even that one dies in.

37

'. . . approached the window as if to see . . .'

The boredom which disclosed
Everything—

I should have written, not the rain
Of a nineteenth century day, but the motes
In the air, the dust

Here still.

What have we argued about? what have we done?

Thickening the air?

Air so thick with myth the words *unlucky*
And *good luck*

Float in it . . .

To 'see' them?

No.

Or sees motes, an iron mesh, links

Of consequence

Still, at the mind's end
Relevant

38

You are the last
Who will know him
Nurse.

Not know him,
He is an old man,
A patient,
How could one know him?

You are the last
Who will see him
Or touch him,
Nurse.

39

Occurring 'neither for self
Nor for truth'

The sad marvels

In the least credible circumstance,
Storm or bombardment

Or the room of a very old man

40

Whitman: 'April 19, 1864

The capitol grows upon one in time, especially as they have
got the great figure on top of it now, and you can see it very
well. It is a great bronze figure, the Genius of Liberty I
suppose. It looks wonderful toward sundown. I love to go and
look at it. The sun when it is nearly down shines on the
headpiece and it dazzles and glistens like a big star: it looks
quite

curious . . .'

• HISTORIC PUN

La petite vie, a young man called it later, it had been the
        last thing offered
In that way,
A way of behaving, a way of being in public
Which we lacked—

If there was doubt it was doubt of himself

Finding a force
In the cafés and bistros

Force of the familiar and familiars
The force of ease

They gather on the steps of Sacré-Coeur,
Great crowds, sitting on the steps
To watch the sunset and the lights—

I speak of tourists. But what we see is there

Find a word for ourselves
Or we will have nothing, neither faith nor will, the will

Touched by the dazzle—

Spring touches the Butte Chaumont,
Every morning the children appear
In the parks,
Paris is beautiful and ludicrous, the leaves of every tree in the
        city move in the wind
The girls have beautiful thighs, beautiful skirts, all simulate
        courage—

Semite: to find a way for myself.

• A KIND OF GARDEN: A POEM FOR MY SISTER

One may say courage
And one may say fear

And nobility
There are women

Radically alone in courage
And fear

Clear minded and blind

In the machines
And the abstractions and the power

Of their times as women can be blind

Untroubled by a leaf moving
In a garden

In mere breeze
Mere cause

But troubled as those are who arrive

Where games have been played
When all games have been won, last difficult garden

Brilliant in courage
Hard clash with the homely

To embellish such victories

Which in that garden
She sought for a friend

Offering gently

A brilliant kindness
Of the brilliant garden

• ROUTE

'the void eternally generative'
the *Wen Fu* of Lu Chi

1

Tell the beads of the chromosomes like a rosary,
Love in the genes, if it fails

We will produce no sane man again

I have seen too many young people become adults, young
    friends become old people, all that is not ours,

The sources
And the crude bone

        —we say

Took place

Like the mass of the hills.

'The sun is a molten mass'. Therefore

Fall into oneself—?

Reality, blind eye
Which has taught us to stare—

Your elbow on a car-edge
Incognito as summer,

I wrote. Not you but a girl
At least

Clarity, clarity, surely clarity is the most beautiful
       thing in the world,
A limited, limiting clarity

I have not and never did have any motive of poetry
But to achieve clarity

2

Troubled that you are not, as they say,
Working—
I think we try rather to understand,
We try also to remain together

There is a force of clarity, it is
Of what is not autonomous in us,
We suffer a certain fear

Things alter, surrounded by a depth
And width

The unreality of our house in moonlight
Is that if the moonlight strikes it
It is truly there tho it is ours

3

Not to reduce the thing to nothing—

I might at the top of my ability stand at a window
and say, look out; out there is the world.

Not the desire for approval nor even for love—O,
that trap! From which escaped, barely—if it fails

We will produce no sane man again

4

Words cannot be wholly transparent. And that is the
        'heartlessness' of words.

Neither friends nor lovers are coeval . . .

as for a long time we have abandoned those in
        extremity and we find it unbearable that we should
        do so . . .

The sea anemone dreamed of something, filtering the sea
        water thru its body,

Nothing more real than boredom—dreamlessness, the
        experience of time, never felt by the new arrival,
        never at the doors, the thresholds, it is the native

Native in native time . . .

The purity of the materials, not theology, but to present
        the circumstances

5

In Alsace, during the war, we found ourselves on the edge of the Battle of the Bulge. The front was inactive, but we were spread so thin that the situation was eerily precarious. We hardly knew where the next squad was, and it was not in sight—a quiet and deserted hill in front of us. We dug in near a farmhouse. Pierre Adam, tho he was a journeyman mason, lived with his wife and his children in that farmhouse.

During the occupation the Germans had declared Alsace a part of Greater Germany. Therefore they had drafted Alsatian men into the German army. Many men, learning in their own way that they were to be called, dug a hole. The word became a part of the language: *faire une trou.* Some men were in those holes as long as two and three years. It was necessary that someone should know where those holes were; in winter it was impossible for a man to come out of his hole without leaving footprints in the snow. While snow was actually falling, however, a friend could come to the hole with food and other help. Pierre, whom many people trusted, knew where some two dozen of those holes were.

The Germans became aware that men were going into hiding, and they began to make reprisals. If the man was young and unmarried, they killed his parents. If the man was married, they took his wife into Germany to the army brothels, it was said. They took the children into Germany, and it was not certain whether those children would remember where they came from. Pierre told me this story:

Men would come to Pierre and they would say: I am thinking of making a hole. Pierre would say: yes. They would say then: but if I do they will kill my parents; or: they will take my wife and my children. Then Pierre would say, he told me: *if* you dig a hole,   I will help you.

He knew, of course, what he was telling me. You must try to put yourself into those times. If one thought he knew anything, it was that a man should not join the Nazi army. Pierre himself learned, shortly before the Americans arrived, that he was about to be drafted. He and his wife discussed the children. They thought of tattooing the children's names and addresses on their chests so that perhaps they could be found after the war. But they thought that perhaps the tattooing would be cut out of the children . . . They did not, finally, have to make that decision, as it turned out. But what a conversation between a man and his wife—

There was an escape from that dilemma, as, in a way, there always is. Pierre told me of a man who, receiving the notification that he was to report to the German army, called a celebration and farewell at his home. Nothing was said at that party that was not jovial. They drank and sang. At the proper time, the host got his bicycle and waved goodbye. The house stood at the top of a hill and, still waving and calling farewells, he rode with great energy and as fast as he could down the hill, and, at the bottom, drove into a tree.

It must be hard to do. Probably easier in an automobile. There is, in an automobile, a considerable time during which you cannot change your mind. Riding a bicycle, since in those woods it is impossible that the tree should be a redwood, it must be necessary to continue aiming at the tree right up to the moment of impact. Undoubtedly difficult to do. And, of course, the children had no father. Thereafter.

6

Wars that are just? A simpler question: In the event,
will you or will you not want to kill a German. Because,
in the event, if you do not want to, you won't.

. . . and my wife reading letters she knew were two weeks
late and did not prove I was not dead while she read. Why
did I play all that, what was I doing there?

We are brothers, we are brothers?—these things are
composed of a moral substance only if they are untrue. If
these things are true they are perfectly simple, perfectly
impenetrable, those primary elements which can only be
named.

A man will give his life for his friend provided he wants
to.

In all probability a man will give his life for his child
provided his child is an infant.

. . . One man could not understand me because I was saying simple things; it seemed to him that nothing was being said. I was saying: there is a mountain, there is a lake

A picture seen from within. The picture is unstable, a moving picture, unlimited drift. Still, the picture exists.

The circumstances:

7

And if at 80

He says what has been commonly said
It is for the sake of old times, a cozy game

He wishes to join again, an unreasonable speech
Out of context

8

Cars on the highway filled with speech,
People talk, they talk to each other;

Imagine a man in the ditch,
The wheels of the overturned wreck
Still spinning—

I don't mean he despairs, I mean if he does not
He sees in the manner of poetry

9

The cars run in a void of utensils
—the powerful tires—beyond
Happiness

Tough rubbery gear of invaders, of the descendents
Of invaders, I begin to be aware of a countryside
And the exposed weeds of a ditch

The context is history
Moving toward the light of the conscious

And beyond, culvert, blind curb, there are also names
For these things, language in the appalling fields

I remember my father as a younger man than I am now,
My mother was a tragic girl
Long ago, the autonomous figures are gone,
The context is the thousands of days

10

Not the symbol but the scene this pavement leads
To roadsides—the finite

Losing its purposes
Is estranged

All this is reportage.

If having come so far we shall have
Song

Let it be small enough.

Virgin
what was there to be thought

comes by the road

11

Tell the life of the mind, the mind creates the finite.

All punishes him. I stumble over these stories—
Progeny, the possibility of progeny, continuity

Or love that tempted him

He is punished by place, by scene, by all that holds
all he has found, this pavement, the silent symbols

Of it, the word it, never more powerful than in this
moment. Well, hardly an epiphany, but there the thing
is all the same

All this is reportage

12

To insist that what is true is good, no matter, no matter,
        a definition—?

That tree
        whose fruit . . .

The weight of air
Measured by the barometer in the parlor,
Time remains what it was

Oddly, oddly insistent

haunting the people in the automobiles,

shining on the sheetmetal,

open and present, unmarred by indifference,

wheeled traffic, indifference,
the hard edge of concrete continually crumbling

into gravel in the gravel of the shoulders,
Ditches of our own country

Whom shall I speak to

13

Department of Plants and Structures—obsolete, the old name
In this city, of the public works

Tho we meant to entangle ourselves in the roots of the world

An unexpected and forgotten spoor, all but indestructible
        shards

To owe nothing to fortune, to chance, nor by the power of
        his heart
Or her heart to have made these things sing
But the benevolence of the real

Tho there is no longer shelter in the earth, round helpless belly
Or hope among the pipes and broken works

'Substance itself which is the subject of all our planning'

And by this we are carried into the incalculable

14

There was no other guarantee

Ours aren't the only madmen tho they have burned thousands
of men and women alive, perhaps no madder than most

Strange to be here, strange for them also, insane and criminal,
who hasn't noticed that, strange to be man, we have come
rather far

We are at the beginning of a radical depopulation of the earth

Cataclysm . . . cataclysm of the plains, jungles, the cities

Something in the soil exposed between two oceans

As Cabeza de Vaca found a continent of spiritual despair
in campsites

His miracles among the Indians heralding cataclysm

Even Cortés greeted as revelation . . . No I'd not emigrate,
I'd not live in a ship's bar wherever we may be headed

These things at the limits of reason, nothing at the limits
of dream, the dream merely ends, by this we know it is the
real

That we confront

• A THEOLOGICAL DEFINITION

A small room, the varnished floor
Making an L around the bed,

What is or is true as
Happiness

Windows opening on the sea,
The green painted railings of the balcony
Against the rock, the bushes and the sea running

• POWER, THE ENCHANTED WORLD

1

Streets, in a poor district—

Crowded,
We mean the rooms

Crowded, they come to stand
In vacant streets

Streets vacant of power

Therefore the irrational roots

We are concerned with the given

2

. . . That come before the swallow dares . . .

The winds of March

Black winds, the gritty winds, mere squalls and rags

There is a force we disregarded and which disregarded us

I'd wanted friends
Who talked of a public justice

Very simple people
I forget what we said

3

Now we do most of the killing
Having found a logic

Which is control
Of the world, 'we'
And Russia

Viet nam

What does it mean to object
Since it will happen?
It is possible, therefore it will happen
And the dead, this time, dead

4

Power, which hides what it can

But within sight of the river

On a wall near a corner marked by the Marylyn Shoppe
And a branch bank

I saw scrawled in chalk the words, Put your hand on your
              heart

And elsewhere, in another hand,

Little Baby Ass

And it is those who find themselves in love with the world /
Who suffer an anguish of mortality

5

Power ruptures at a thousand holes
Leaking the ancient air in,

The paraphernalia of a culture
On the gantries

And the grease of the engine itself
At the extremes of reality

Which was not what we wanted

The heart uselessly opens
To 3 words, which is too little

- BALLAD

Astrolabes and lexicons
Once in the great houses—

A poor lobsterman

Met by chance
On Swan's Island

Where he was born
We saw the old farmhouse

Propped and leaning on its hilltop
On that island
Where the ferry runs

A poor lobsterman

His teeth were bad

He drove us over that island
In an old car

A well-spoken man

Hardly real
As he knew in those rough fields

Lobster pots and their gear
Smelling of salt

The rocks outlived the classicists,
The rocks and the lobstermen's huts

And the sights of the island
The ledges in the rough sea seen from the road

And the harbor
And the post office

Difficult to know what one means
—to be serious and to know what one means—

An island
Has a public quality

His wife in the front seat

In a soft dress
Such as poor women wear

She took it that we came—
I don't know how to say, she said—

Not for anything we did, she said,
Mildly, 'from God'. She said

What I like more than anything
Is to visit other islands . . .

- SEASCAPE: NEEDLE'S EYE

- FROM A PHRASE OF SIMONE WEIL'S
  AND SOME WORDS OF HEGEL'S

In   back   deep the jewel
The treasure
No   Liquid
Pride of the living life's liquid
Pride in the sandspit wind this ether this other this element all
It is I or I believe
We are the beaks of the ragged birds
Tune of the ragged bird's beaks
In the tune of the winds
Ob via   the obvious
Like a fire of straws
Aflame in the world or else poor people hide
Yourselves together   Place
Place where   desire
Lust of the eyes the pride of life and foremost of the storm's
Multitude moves the wave belly-lovely
Glass of the glass sea shadow of water
On the open water no other way
To come here the outer
Limit of the ego

Limited air   drafts
In the treasure house moving and the movements of the living
Things fall   something balanced   Move
With all one's force
Into the commonplace that pierces or erodes

The mind's structure but nothing
Incredible happens
It will have happened to that other
The survivor . The survivor
To him it happened .

Rooted in basalt
Night hums like the telephone dial tone blue gauze
Of the forge flames the pulse
Of infant
Sorrows at the crux

Of the timbers
When the middle Kingdom
Warred with beasts Middle Things the elves the

Magic people in their world
Among the plant roots   hopes
Which are the hopes
Of small self interest called

Superstition chitinous
Toys of the children wings
Of the wasp.

• ANIMULA

animula blandula vagula

Chance and chance and thereby starlit
All that was to be thought
Yes
Comes down the road   Air of the waterfronts   black air

Over the iron bollard   the doors cracked

In the starlight things the things continue
Narrative   their long instruction and the tide running
Strong as a tug's wake   shorelights'

Fractured dances across rough water a music ,
Who would believe it,
Not quite one's own ,
With one always the black verse   the turn and the turn

At the lens' focus   the crystal pool   innavigable

Torrent, torment Eden's
Flooded valley   dramas

Of dredged waters
A wind blowing out

And out to sea   the late the salt times cling

In panicked
Spirals at the hull's side sea's streaks floating
Curved on the sea little pleasant soul wandering

Frightened

The small mid-ocean
Moon lights the winches

● WEST

Elephant, say, scraping its dry sides
In a narrow place as he passes says yes

This is true

So one knows?   and the ferns unfurling   leaves

In the wind

. . . sea   from which . .

'We address the future?   '

Unsure of the times
Unsure I can answer

To myself   We have been ignited
Blazing

In wrath we await

The rare poetic
Of veracity that huge art whose geometric
Light seems not its own in that most dense world West
        and East
Have denied have hated have wandered in   *precariousness*

Like a new fire

Will burn out the roots
One thinks of steep fields
Of brown grass
In the mountains it seems they lie

Aslant in the thin
Burning air and among clouds the sun
Passes boulders   grass blades   sky clad things

In nakedness
Inseparable   *the children will say*

Our parents waited in the woods   *precarious*

Transparent as the childhood of the world
Growing old   the seagulls sound like the voices of children
          wilder than children wildest of children the waves'
          riot
Brilliant as the world
Up side down   Not obstinate islands

This is the seaboard   New skilled fishermen
In the great bays and the narrow bights

' . . . as if a nail whose wide head
were time and space . . '

at the nail's point the hammer-blow
undiminished

Holes   pitfalls open
In the cop's accoutrement

Crevasse

The destitute metal

Jail metal

Impoverished   Intimate
As a Father did you know that

Old friend   old poet
Tho you'd walked

Familiar streets
And glittered with change the circle

Destroyed its content
Persists   the common

Place   image
The initial light   Walk on the walls

The walls of the fortress   the countryside
Broad in the night light the sap rises

Out of obscurities the sap rises
The sap not exhausted   Movement
Of the stone   Music
Of the tenement

Also is this lonely theme   Earth
My sister

Lonely sister my sister but why did I weep
Meeting that poet again what was that rage

Before Leger's art poster
In war time Paris perhaps art

Is one's mother and father   O rage
Of the exile   Fought ice

Fought shifting stones
Beyond the battlement

Crevasse   Fought

No man
But the fragments of metal
Tho there were men there were men   Fought
No man but the fragments of metal
Burying my dogtag with H
For Hebrew in the rubble of Alsace

I must get out of here

Father   he thinks   *father*

Disgrace of dying

Old friend   old poet
If you did not look

What is it you 'loved'
Twisting your voice   your walk

Wet roads

Hot sun on the hills

He walks twig-strewn streets
Of the rain

Walks homeward

Unteachable

• SONG, THE WINDS OF DOWNHILL

'out of poverty
to begin

again'   impoverished

of tone of pose that common
wealth

of parlance   Who
so poor the words

would   with   and   take on substantial

meaning   handholds   footholds

to dig in one's heels   sliding

hands and heels beyond the residential
lots   the plots   it is a poem

which may be sung
may well be sung

1

Moving over the hills, crossing the irrigation
canals perfect and profuse in the mountains the
streams of women and men walking under the high-
tension wires over the brown hills

                    in the multiple world of the fly's
multiple eye the songs they go to hear on
this occasion are no one's own

Needle's eye   needle's eye   but in the ravine
again and again on the massive spike the song
clangs

as the tremendous volume of the music takes
over obscured by their long hair they seem
to be mourning

A MORALITY PLAY: PREFACE

Lying full length
On the bed in the white room

Turns her eyes to me

Again,

Naked . .

Never to forget her naked eyes

Beautiful and brave
Her naked eyes

Turn inward

Feminine light

The unimagined
Feminine light

Feminine ardor

Pierced and touched

Tho all say
Huddled among each other

'Love'

The play begins with the world

A city street
Leads to the bay

· 215

Tamalpais in cloud

Mist over farmlands

Local knowledge
In the heavy hills

The great loose waves move landward
Heavysided in the wind

Grass and trees bent
Along the length of coast in the continual wind

The ocean pounds in her mind
Not the harbor leading inward
To the back bay and the slow river
Recalling flimsy Western ranches
The beautiful hills shine outward

Sunrise   the raw fierce fire
Coming up past the sharp edge

And the hoof marks on the mountain

Shines in the white room

Provincial city
Not alien enough

To naked eyes

This city died young

You too will be shown this

You will see the young couples

Leaving again in rags

3

So with artists.   How pleasurable
to imagine that, if only they gave
up their art, the children would be
healed,   would live.

                    Irving Younger in *The Nation*

'AND THEIR WINTER AND NIGHT IN DISGUISE'

The sea and a crescent strip of beach
Show between the service station and a deserted shack

A creek drains thru the beach
Forming a ditch
There is a discarded super-market cart in the ditch
That beach is the edge of a nation

There is something like shouting along the highway
A California shouting
On the long fast highway over the California mountains

Point Pedro
Its distant life

It is impossible the world should be either good or bad
If its colors are beautiful or if they are not beautiful
If parts of it taste good or if no parts of it taste good
It is as remarkable in one case as the other
                                        As against this

We have suffered fear, we know something of fear
And of humiliation mounting to horror

The world above the edge of the foxhole belongs to the
        flying bullets, leaden superbeings
For the men grovelling in the foxhole danger, danger in
        being drawn to them

These little dumps
The poem is about them

Our hearts are twisted
In dead men's pride

Dead men crowd us
Lean over us

In the emplacements

The skull spins
Empty of subject

The hollow ego

Flinching from the war's huge air

Tho we are delivery boys and bartenders

We will choke on each other

Minds may crack

But not for what is discovered

Unless that everyone knew
And kept silent

Our minds are split
To seek the danger out

From among the miserable soldiers

4

ANNIVERSARY POEM

        'the picturesque
common lot' the unwarranted light

Where everyone has been

The very ground of the path
And the litter grow ancient

A shovel's scratched edge
So like any other man's

We are troubled by incredulity
We are troubled by scratched things

Becoming familiar
Becoming extreme

Let grief
Be
So it be ours

Nor hide one's eyes
As tides drop along the beaches in the thin wash of
                breakers

And so desert each other

—lest there be nothing

        The Indian girl walking across the desert, the
sunfish under the boat

How shall we say how this happened, these stories, our
            stories

Scope, mere size, a kind of redemption

Exposed still and jagged on the San Francisco hills

Time and depth before us, paradise of the real, we
                know what it is

To find now depth, not time, since we cannot, but depth

To come out safe,   to end well

We have begun to say good bye
To each other
And cannot say it

5

The Translucent Mechanics

Combed thru the piers the wind
Moves in the clever city
Not in the doors but the hinges
Finds the secret of motion
As tho the hollow ships moved in their voices,   murmurs
Flaws
In the wind
Fear   fear
At the lumber mastheads
And fetched a message out of the sea again

Say angel   say powers

Obscurely   'things
And the self'

Prosody

Sings

In the stones

        to entrust
To a poetry of statement

At close quarters

A living mind
'and that one's own'

                what then   what spirit

Of the bent seas

Archangel

of the tide
brimming

in the moon-streak

          comes in whose absence
earth crumbles

6

Silver as
The needle's eye

Of the horizon in the noise
Of their entrance row on row the waves
Move landward   conviction's

Net of branches
In the horde of events the sacred swarm avalanche
Masked in the sunset

Needle after needle more numerous than planets

Or the liquid waves
In the tide rips

We believe   we believe

Beyond the cable car streets
And the picture window

Lives the glittering crumbling night
Of obstructions and the stark structures

That carry wires over the mountain
One writes in the presence of something
Moving close to fear
I dare pity no one
Let the rafters pity
The air in the room
Under the rafters
Pity
In the continual sound
Are chords
Not yet struck
Which will be struck
Nevertheless yes

7

O withering seas
Of the doorstep and local winds unveil

The face of art

Carpenter, plunge and drip in the sea   Art's face
We know that face

More blinding than the sea   a haunted house   a limited

Consensus unwinding

Its powers
Toward the thread's end

In the record of great blows   shocks
Ravishment   devastation   the wood splintered

The keyboard gone in the rank grass swept her hand
Over the strings and the thing rang out

Over the rocks and the ocean
Not my poem   Mr Steinway's

Poem   Not mine   A 'marvelous' object
Is not the marvel of things

        twisting the new
Mouth   forcing the new
Tongue   But it rang

8

The Taste

Old ships are preserved
For their queer silence of obedient seas
Their cutwaters floating in the still water
With their cozy black iron work
And Swedish seamen dead   the cabins
Hold the spaces of their deaths
And the hammered nails of necessity
Carried thru the oceans
Where the moon rises grandly
In the grandeur of cause
We have a taste for bedrock
Beneath this spectacle
To gawk at ,
Something is wrong with the antiques, a black fluid
Has covered them, a black splintering
Under the eyes of young wives
People talk wildly, we are beginning to talk wildly, the wind
At every summit
Our overcoats trip us
Running for the bus
Our arms stretched out
In a wind from what were sand dunes

· 225

9

THE IMPOSSIBLE POEM

Climbing the peak of Tamalpais the loose
Gravel underfoot

And the city shining with the tremendous wrinkles
In the hills and the winding of the bay
Behind it, it faces the bent ocean

Streetcars
Rocked thru the city and the winds
Combed their clumsy sides

In clumsy times

Sierras withering
Behind the storefronts

And sanity the roadside weed
Dreams of sports and sportsmanship

In the lucid towns paralyzed
Under the truck tires
Shall we relinquish

Sanity to redeem
Fragments and fragmentary
Histories in the towns and the temperate streets
Too shallow still to drown in or to mourn
The courageous and precarious children

10

BUT SO AS BY FIRE

The darkness of trees
Guards this life
Of the thin ground
That covers the rock ledge

Among the lanes and magic
Of the Eastern woods

The beauty of silence
And broken boughs

And the homes of small animals

The green leaves
Of young plants
Above the dark green moss
In the sweet smell of rot

The pools and the trickle of freshwater

First life,   rotting life
Hidden starry life it is not yet

A mirror
Like our lives

We have gone
As far as is possible

Whose lives reflect light
Like mirrors

One had not thought
To be afraid

Not of shadow but of light

Summon one's powers

- EXODUS

children of Israel

Miracle of the children   the brilliant
Children   the word
Liquid as woodlands   Children?

When she was a child I read Exodus
To my daughter   'The children of Israel . . .'

Pillar of fire
Pillar of cloud

We stared at the end
Into each other's eyes ,   Where
She said hushed

Were the adults ?   We dreamed to each other
Miracle of the children
The brilliant children   Miracle

Of their brilliance   Miracle
of

- MYTH OF THE BLAZE

• LATITUDE, LONGITUDE

     climbed from the road and found
over the flowers at the mountain's
rough top a bee yellow
and heavy as

       pollen in the mountainous
air thin legs crookedly
a-dangle if we could

find all
the gale's evidence what message
is there for us in these
glassy bottles the Encyclopedist

was wrong was wrong many things
too foolish
to sing
may be said this matter-
of-fact defines

poetry

• THE SPEECH AT SOLI

what do you want
to tell while the world

speaks nights or some nights
sleepless

fearful remembering
myself in these towns or by car

thru these towns   unconscionable

adolescent young girls fall into wells

says a letter

bringing to birth

in the green storm

anger.   anger,
and the light of the self small
blazing sun of the farms—   return

the return of the sun there are actors'

faces of the highways the theatre
greets itself and reverberates the spirit
goes down goes under
stationary
valves of ditches the chartered
rivers threats in stones
enemies in sidewalks and when the stars rise
reverse ourselves regions of the mind

alter
mad kings

gone raving

war in incoherent
sunlight it will not

cohere it will NOT that
other

desertion
of the total we discover

Friday's footprint is it as the sun moves

beyond the blunt
towns of the coast   fishermen's

tumbled tumbling headlands the needle silver
water, and tells the public time

● THE BOOK OF JOB AND A DRAFT OF A POEM TO PRAISE THE PATHS OF THE LIVING

in memory of Mickey Schwerner

image   the images   the great games therefore the locked

the half-lit jailwinds

in the veins the lynch gangs

simulate blows   bruise   the bones
breaking   *age*

of the world's deeds this is the young age   age

of the sea's surf   image   image

of the world its least rags
stream among the planets   Our
lady of poverty the lever the fulcrum
the cam and the ant
hath her anger and the emmet
his choler the exposed
belly of the land
under the sky
at night and the windy pines unleash
the morning's force what is the form
to say it there is something
to name Goodman   Schwerner   Chaney
who were beaten not we
who were beaten   children
not our
children   ancestral
children rose in the dark
to their work there grows

there builds there is written
a vividness   there is   rawness
like a new sun the flames
tremendous the sun
itself ourselves ourselves
go with us *disorder*

so great the tumult wave

upon wave this traverse

this desert   extravagant
island of light

●   ●

the long road
going north

on the cliffs   small
and numerous

the windows

look out on the sea's simulacra
of self-evidence   meaning's

instant   wild-
eyed as the cherry
tree blossoms

in that fanatic glass from our own
homes our own

rooms we are fetched out   we

the greasers
says yesterday's

slang in the path of tornado the words

piled on each other   lean
on each other dance

with the dancing

valve stems   machine glint
in the commonplace the last words

survivors, will be tame
will stand near our feet
what shall we say   they have lived their lives
they have gone feathery
and askew
in the wind from the beginning   carpenter
mechanic   o we
impoverished we hired
hands that turn the wheel   young
theologians of the scantlings   wracked
monotheists of the   weather-side   sometimes I imagine
they speak

        •   •

luxury,   all
said Bill, the fancy things   always

second hand but in extreme
minutes guilt

at the heart
of the unthinkable hunger   fear   enemy

world   briefly shame

of loneliness all that has touched
the man

• 238

touches him
again arms and dis-

arms him meaning
in the instant

tho we forget

the light

●   ●

precision of place the rock's place in the fog we suffer
        loneliness painlessly not without fear the common breath
            here at extremity

obsolescent as the breathing
of tribespeople   fingers cold

early in the year cold and windy on the sea the wind
        still blows thru my head in the farmhouse

weather of the camera's click
lonely as the shutter closing
over the glass lens weathered mountains

of the hurrying sea the boat in these squalls sails
        like a sparrow a wind blown
sparrow on the sea some kite string

taut in the wind green
and heavy the masses of the sea weeds move
and move in rock shelters share marvelous games

●   ●

inshore,   the rough grasses
rooted on the dry hills or to stand still

like the bell buoy   telling

tragedy so wide
spread so

shabby a north sea salt
tragedy 'seeking a statement

of an experience of our own' the bones of my hands

bony   bony   lose me the wind cries   find
yourself   I?

this?   the road
and the travelling   always

undiscovered
country forever

savage *the river*
was a rain and flew

with the herons   the sea
flies in the squall

• •

backward
over the shoulder
now the wave
of the improbable
drains from the beaches the heart of the hollow
tree singing bird note bird rustle we live now
in dreams all

wished to tell him we are locked
in ourselves   That is not
what they dreamed
in any dream they dreamed the weird morning
of the bird waking mid continent

mid continent iron rails
in the fields and grotesque
metals in the farmer's heartlands a sympathy
across the fields
and down the aisles
of the crack trains
of 1918 the wave
of the improbable
drenches the galloping carpets in the sharp
edges in the highlights
of the varnished tables we ring
in the continual bell
the undoubtable bell found music   in itself
of itself speaks the word
actual heart breaking
tone row it is not ended
not ended the intervals
blurred ring
like walls
between floor
and ceiling the taste
of madness in the world   birds
of ice   Pave
the world o pave
the world carve

thereon . .

• MYTH OF THE BLAZE

night – sky   bird's   world
to know   to know   in my life to know

what I have said to myself

the dark to escape in brilliant highways
of the night sky, finally
why had they not

killed me why did they fire that warning
wounding cannon only the one round I hold a
      superstition

because of this   lost to be lost   Wyatt's
lyric and Rezi's
running thru my mind
in the destroyed (and guilty) Theatre
of the War   I'd cried
and remembered
boyhood   degradation   other
degradations and this crime I will not recover
from that landscape it will be in my mind
it will fill my mind and this is horrible
death bed   pavement   the secret taste
of being lost

dead

clown in the birds'
world what names
(but my name)

and my love's name to speak

into the eyes
of the Tyger   blaze

of changes . . . 'named

the animals'   name

and name the vigorous dusty strong

animals gather
under the joists   the boards   older

than they   giving
them darkness the gifted

dark tho names   the names   the 'little'

adventurous
words   a mountain   the cliff

a wave are taxonomy I believe

in the world

because it is
impossible   the shack

on the coast

under the eaves
the rain barrel flooding

in the weather and no lights

across rough water illumined
as tho the narrow

end of the funnel what are the names
of the Tyger   to speak
to the eyes

of the Tiger   blaze
of the tiger   who moves in the forest leaving

no scent

but the pine needles' his eyes blink

quick
in   the shack
in the knife-cut
and the opaque

white

bread each side of the knife

• INLET

Mary in the noisy seascape
Of the whitecaps

Of another people's summer
Talked of the theologians   so brave
In the wilderness she said ,   and off the town pier

Rounding that heavy coast of mountains
The night drifts
Over the rope's end

Glass world

Glass heaven

Brilliant beneath the boat's round bilges
In the surface of the water
Shepherds are good people let them sing .

the little skirts life's breasts for what we can have
Is each other

Breath of the barnacles
Over England

over ocean

breakwaters   hencoops

- **SEMITE**

what art and anti-art to lead us by the sharpness

of its definitions connected
to all other things this is the bond

sung to all distances

my distances neither Roman

nor barbarian the sky the low sky

of poems precise
as the low sky

that women have sung from the windows
of cities sun's light

on the sills a poetry

of the narrow
end of the funnel proximity's salt gales in the narrow

end of the funnel the proofs

are the images the images
overwhelming earth

rises up

in its light nostalgia
of the mud guilts

of the foxhole what is a word a name at the
limits

of devotion
to life the terrible knowledge

of deception

a lie told my loves tragically
pitifully had deceived

themselves had been betrayed

demeaned thrown away shamed
degraded

stripped naked Think

think also of the children
the guards laughing

the one pride the pride
of the warrior laughing so the hangman
comes to all dinners Aim

we tell each other the children cannot be
        alone whereupon murder

comes to our dinners poem born

of a planet the size

of a table top
garden   forest   an awning

fluttering four-lane

highway the instant

in the open the moving
edge and one
is I

• THE LITTLE PIN: FRAGMENT

*'The journey fortunately [said the traveller] is
truly immense'*

of this
all things
speak if they speak the estranged

unfamiliar sphere thin as air
of rescue   huge

pin-point

cold little pin unresting
small pin of the wind and the rayne

in the fields the pines the spruces the sea and
        the intricate

veins in the stones and the rock
of the mountains wandering

stars in the dark their one
moral in the breeze

of wherever it is history
goes the courses and breaking

High seas of history . . . . Stagecraft
Statecraft the cast is absurd the seas
break on the beaches

of labor multitudinous
beach and the long cost

of dishonest
music

       Song?

astonishing

song?   the world
sometime be

world the wind
be wind o western
wind to speak

      of this

• THE LIGHTHOUSES

(for L Z in time of the breaking of nations)

if you want to say no say
no if you want to say yes say yes in loyalty

to all fathers or joy
of escape

from all my fathers I want to say

yes and say
yes the turning
lights

of oceans in which to say what one knows and to
limit oneself to this

knowledge is

loneliness turning and turning

lights

of safety for the coasts

are danger rock-pierced
fatalities far out   far out the structures

of cause

and consequence silver as
the minnows'

flash miraculous

as the seed sprouting
green at my feet among a distant

people therefore run away,
into everything the gift

the treasure is

flight my
heritage *neither Roman*

nor barbarian now the walls are

falling the turn the cadence the verse

and the music essential

clarity plain glass ray
of darkness ray of light

• CONFESSION

'neither childhood
nor future

are growing less' guilts   guilts
pour in

to memory things leak I am an old ship
and leaky   oceans

in the bilges ordinary

oceans in the bilges I come to know it is so guilts
        guilts

failures in the creaking
timbers but to have touched

foundations keelson the cellars
as all this becomes strange

enough
I come to know it is home a groping

down a going
down middle-voice the burgeoning

desolate   magic   the dark
grain

of sand and eternity

• WHO SHALL DOUBT

consciousness

      in itself

of itself carrying

    'the principle
        of the actual' being

actual

itself ((but maybe this is a love
poem

Mary)) nevertheless

      neither

the power
of the self nor the racing
car nor the lilly

      is sweet but this

• TO THE POETS: TO MAKE MUCH OF LIFE

'come up now into
the world' no need to light

the lamps in daylight *that passion
that light within*

and without   (the old men were dancing

return
the return of the sun)   no need to light

lamps in daylight working year
after
year the poem

discovered

in the crystal
center of the rock image

and image the transparent

present tho we speak of the abyss
of the hungry we see their feet their tired

feet in the news and mountain and valley
and sea as in universal

storm
the fathers said we are old
we are shrivelled

come.

• TWO ROMANCE POEMS

(for Jeremy Taylor)

something wrong with my desk   the desk
the destroyer, desk is the enemy

bright light of shipwreck beautiful as the sea
and the islands I don't know how to say it
needing a word with no sound

but the pebbles shifting on the beach the sense
of the thing, everything, rises in the mind the
venture   adventure

say as much as I dare, as much as I can
sustain I don't know how to say it

I say all that I can   What one would tell
would be the scene   Again!!   power

of the scene I said the small paved area,
ordinary ground except that it is high above
the city, the people standing at a little distance
from each other, or in small groups

would be the poem

If one wrote it   No heroics, obviously, but
the sadness takes on another look

as tho it mattered, in a way
'smoke drifts from our hills'

•   •

Res Publica: 'The Poets Lie'

words, the words older
than I

clumsiest

of poets the rain's small

pellets   small

fountains that live
on the face

of the waters

dilations

of the heart they say
too much the heart the
heart of the republic skips

a beat where they touch it

- INDEX OF TITLES AND FIRST LINES

• INDEX OF TITLES AND FIRST LINES

A city of the corporations, 94
A friend saw the rooms, 104
Against the glass, 51
Ah these are the poor, 109
A Kind of Garden: A Poem for My Sister, 182
A Language of New York, 94
Alpine, 116
Also he has set the world, 21
A Morality Play: Preface, 215
Amor fati, 151
A Narrative, 132
'. . . and her closets!' 122
And if at 80, 190
And the child, 122
'And Their Winter and Night in Disguise,' 217
And the world changed, 60
And truth? O, 133
And war, 32
'and you too, old man . . . ,' 102
An enclave, 135
Animula, 207
Anniversary Poem, 219
Antique, 51
'approached the window as if to see . . . ,' 177
Armies of the Plain, 73
'. . . as if a nail whose wide head,' 210
As I saw, 10
A small room, the varnished floor, 197
As the builders, 63
Astrolabes and lexicons, 201
A Theological Definition, 197
A woman dreamed, 115
A world around her like a shadow, 53
'A zero, a nothing,' 73

Bad times, 13
Bahamas, 113
Ballad, 201
Because he could not face, 114

Because the known and the unknown, 172
Behind their house, behind the back porch, 172
Beyond the Hudson's, 42
Birthplace: New Rochelle, 34
Blood from the Stone, 31
Bolt, 10
Boy's Room, 104
But at night the park, 138
But no screen would show, 25
But So As by Fire, 227

California, 62
Carpenter's Boat, 110
Carrying their deckhands' bicycles, 48
Cars on the highway filled with speech, 191
Cell by cell the baby made herself, the cells, 30
Chance and chance and thereby starlit, 207
Chartres, 56
Children of the early, 105
Chorus (androgynous): 'Find me,' 158
Civil war photo, 9
Clarity, 162
climbed from the road and found, 233
Climbing the peak of Tamalpais the loose, 226
Closed car—closed in glass——, 6
Coastal Strip, 52
Combed thru the piers the wind, 221
'come up now into,' 254
coming about, 61
Confession, 252
consciousness, 253

Daedalus: The Dirge, 58
Deaths everywhere——, 14

Debt, 39
Department of Plants and Structures . . . , 195
Down-town, 45
Drawing, 14

Eclogue, 17
Elephant, say, scraping its dry sides, 208
Endlessly, endlessly, 19
Eric—we used to call him Eric—, 50
Eros, 102
Exodus, 229

Failure, worse failure, nothing seen, 143
Fifty years, 33
Five Poems about Poetry, 80
Flight, 128
For love we all go, 112
For the people of that flow, 149
Fragonard, 12
From a Photograph, 47
From a Phrase of Simone Weil's and Some Words of Hegel's, 205
From Disaster, 29
From this distance thinking toward you, 10
From Virgil, 84

Giovanni's Rape of the Sabine Women *at Wildenstein's,* 91
Guest Room, 87

'Half free,' 163
Her ankles are watches, 5
Her arms around me—child—, 47
Her breasts, 130
Historic Pun, 180
How we loved them, 125

I am the father of no country, 132
I believe my apprenticeship, 141
I cannot even now, 96, 157
If the city has roots, they are in filth, 55
if you want to say no say, 250
Image of the Engine, 18

image the images the great games . . . , 236
Impossible to doubt the world: it can be seen, 83
In Alsace, during the war . . . , 187
In back deep the jewel, 205
Inlet, 245
In the door, 15
'In these explanations . . . ,' 155
In the small beauty of the forest, 78
In this nation, 164
I remember a square of New York's Hudson River . . . , 49
I saw from the bus, 136
I, says the buzzard, 84
It brightens up into the branches, 13
It is a place, 136
It is difficult now to speak of poetry—, 168
it is *that* light, 153
It is the air of atrocity, 160

La petite vie, a young man called it later . . . , 180
Latitude, Longitude, 233
Leaving the house each dawn I see the hawk, 41
Leviathan, 68
Like a flat sea, 22
Likely as not a ruined head gasket, 18
Like the wind in the trees and the bells, 174
Limited air drafts, 206
Lying full length, 215

Mary in the noisy seascape, 245
Me! he says, hand on his chest, 35
Miracle of the children the brilliant, 229
Monument, 127
Moving over the hills, crossing the irrigation, 214
My daughter, my daughter, what can I say, 170
Myself I Sing, 35
Myth of the Blaze, 242

Near your eyes——, 11
'neither childhood,' 252
Niece, 129
Night Scene, 118
night–sky   bird's   world, 242
No interval of manner, 12
Not by growth, 14
Not the symbol but the scene . . . , 192
Not to reduce the thing to nothing ——, 186
Now in the helicopters the casual will, 160
Now we do most of the killing, 199

Obsessed, bewildered, 151
Occurring 'neither for self,' 179
'O city ladies,' 12
Of Being Numerous, 147
Of Hours, 210
of this, 248
Of This All Things . . . , 111
Old ships are preserved, 225
One imagines himself, 142
One may say courage, 182
Only that it should be beautiful, 173
On that water, 20
On the water, solid——, 13
. . . or define, 175
Or, in that light, New Arts! . . . , 153
'out of poverty,' 213
Outside the porthole life, or what is, 128
O Western Wind, 53
O withering seas, 224
Ozymandias, 38

Parked in the fields, 86
Parousia, 83
Part of the Forest, 59
Party on Shipboard, 8
Pedestrian, 64
Penobscot, 105
Philai te kou philai, 75
Poor savages, 119
Population, 22
Possible, 97

Power ruptures at a thousand holes, 200
Power, the Enchanted World, 198
Power, which hides what it can, 199
Primitive, 115
Product, 40
Pro Nobis, 141
Psalm, 78
Public silence indeed is nothing, 127

Quotations, 122

Rationality, 117
Rectangular, rearing, 44
Red Hook: December, 124
Resort, 23
Return, 26
Returning to that house, 34
River of our substance, 140
Route, 184
Ruby's day, 74

Sara in Her Father's Arms, 30
Seated Man, 108
Semaphoring chorus, 8
Semite, 246
Serpent, Ouroboros, 137
She lies, hip high, 9
Showing the girl, 91
Silver as, 223
Sing like a bird at the open, 82
Solution, 24
Some of the young men, 139
Someone has scrawled, 123
Some San Francisco Poems, 214
something wrong with my desk the desk, 255
Song, the Winds of Downhill, 213
So spoke of the existence of things, 148
Sparrow in the cobbled street, 37
Squall, 61
Still Life, 67
Stranger's Child, 37
Strange that the youngest people I know, 100, 164
Street, 109
Streets, in a poor district—, 198

Sunnyside Child, 63
Survival: Infantry, 60

Technologies, 71
Tell the beads of the chromosomes . . . , 184
Tell the life of the mind . . . , 193
. . . That come before the swallow dares . . . , 198
That Land, 82
That 'part,' 39
That this is I, 54
The Bicycles and the Apex, 125
The Book of Job and a Draft of a Poem to Praise the Paths of the Living, 236
The boy accepted them, 58
The Building of the Skyscraper, 131
The bulk of it, 56
The cars run in a void of utensils, 191
The City of Keansburg, 79
The constant singing, 134
The Crowded Countries of the Bomb, 57
The darkness of trees, 227
The drunken man, 118
The edge of the ocean, 9
The emotions are engaged, 149
The evening, water in a glass, 4
The five, 38
The Forms of Love, 86
The Founder, 114
The Gesture, 80
The great stone, 150
The headland towers over ocean, 62
The heart pounds, 45
The Hills, 54
The householder issuing to the street, 46
The Impossible Poem, 226
The infants and the animals, 122
The knowledge not of sorrow, you were, 3
The land runs in a flat strip . . . , 52
The light, 169
The Lighthouses, 250

The lights, 138
The lights that blaze and promise, 43
The Little Hole, 81
The little hole in the eye, 81
The Little Pin: Fragment, 248
The man is old and—, 108
The mast, 6
The Mayan Ground, 119
The Men of Sheepshead, 50
The men talking, 17
The new wood as old as carpentry, 110
The Occurrences, 126, 206
The People, the People, 112
'the picturesque,' 219
The puzzle assembled, 24
The question is: how does one hold an apple, 80
There are lovers who recall that, 59
There are the feminine aspects, 111
There are things, 147
There can be a brick, 99, 162
There is a portrait by Eakins, 75
There is in age, 87
There is no beauty in New England like the boats, 40
There is no 'cure,' 117
There's a volcano snow-capped in the air . . . , 23
There was no other guarantee, 196
The roots of words, 159
The sea and a crescent strip of beach, 217
These are the small resorts, 79
The simplest, 126
The solitary are obsessed, 44
The Source, 55
The Speech at Soli, 234
The steel worker on the girder, 131
The streets of San Francisco, 129
The Taste, 225
The Thirties. And, 31
The three wide, 5
The Translucent Mechanics, 221
The Tugs of Hull, 48

The Undertaking in New Jersey, 42
—They await, 161
They carry nativeness, 165
The Zulu Girl, 130
This Earth the king said, 26
This land, 8
Tho in a sort of summer the hard buds blossom, 71
Tho the world, 176
Time of the Missile, 49
To C.T., 142
To insist that what is true is good . . . , 194
To Memory, 65
To the Poets: To Make Much of Life, 254
Tourist Eye, 43
Town, a town, 11
Travelogue, 25
Troubled that you are not, as they say, 185
Truth also is the pursuit of it, 68
Tug against the river——, 9
Two Romance Poems, 255

Ultimately the air, 29
unable to begin, 95, 156

Vulcan, 46

Wars that are just? A simpler question . . . , 189
Wave in the round of the port-hole, 8
We are pressed, pressed on each other, 150
We had not expected it, the whole street, 124
West, 208
We were hiding, 116
What *are* you, apple! There are men, 67
what art and anti-art to lead us . . . , 246
what do you want, 234
What ends, 20
What generations could have dreamed, 64
What man could do, 57
When I asked the very old man, 122
Where are we, 113
'Whether, as the intensity of see-ing increases . . . ,' 152
Which act is, 98
Which is ours, which is ourselves, 173
White, From the, 3
Whitman: 'April 19, 1864,' 101, 179
Who but the Goddess? All that is, 65
Who comes is occupied, 7
Who Shall Doubt, 253
Words cannot be wholly trans-parent . . . , 186
Words, there are words!, 66
Workman, 41
World, World——, 143
Written structure, 14

You are the last, 178